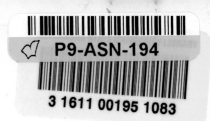

AIR TRAVEL
a Social History

AIR TRAVEL

a Social History by *Kenneth Hudson*

ROWMAN AND LITTLEFIELD
TOTOWA, NEW JERSEY

© 1972 Kenneth Hudson
First published in 1972 by Rowman and Littlefield, Totowa, N.J.
ISBN 0–87471–153–3
Printed and bound in Great Britain by Butler & Tanner Ltd, Frome and London

Contents

5

List of Illustrations

Acknowledgements

AMONG the many institutions and individuals who have helped me during research for this book, I should like to record my particular thanks to the following:

Aeroflot; Dr Gert Behrsing (Lufthansa); Captain Lester Brain (Qantas); R. A. Bruce (Air-India); R. Chagnot (Air France); P. Dunch (Qantas); Charles Gibbs-Smith; R. J. Gibson (Qantas); A. Hone (KLM); The Insurance Institute of London; Fried. Krupp, GmbH; Mardon, Son & Hall, Bristol; L. J. McDonald (Pilkington Bros); Musée de l'Air, Paris; National Air & Space Museum, Washington; National Library of Ireland; A. Nayler, Librarian, Royal Aeronautical Society; R. W. Orme (Loftleidir); W. Palham (Lufthansa); Pan American World Airways, New York; H. Scanlan (*Shell Aviation News*); T. Scott-Chard (BOAC); M. G. Seydel (Sabena); Captain Henry Shaw; John A. F. Till (Air France); Trans-World Airlines, New York; G. Tudor (Japan Air Lines); T. Woodhams (United Arab Airlines) and F. Zandvliet (KLM).

A large correspondence and a considerable part of the library and archive research was carried out by Ann Nicholls. I am very grateful to her for this, and for gathering together the wide range of photographs from which those reproduced here have been selected. I am also much indebted to Amanda Harty for her skill and patience in extracting information from veteran airline passengers.

Foreword

THE HISTORY of aviation has been written many times and in many languages, and this book makes no attempt to perform the task once again. The technology, the pilots, the airlines and the politics have been admirably served by other writers. The present aim is more specialised: to concentrate on the passengers, who appear to have been rather ignored so far, and to discover what the various airlines have done to recruit, please, flatter and subdue them over half a century of operations. The process of change is still continuous, of course, and the final chapter contains suggestions as to the way things are likely to go during what remains of the twentieth century.

The material has been brought together from many sources – the archives and house journals of the airlines, newspapers and periodicals, novels, biographies, memoirs, travel books, autobiographies and interviews with a large number of people who flew as fare-paying passengers at one time or another. Wherever possible, contemporary material has been allowed to speak for itself, since to paraphrase or summarise it is usually to destroy its flavour and lessen its impact.

1 Popularising the flying idea. Daisy Lukens, parachutist and member of the Great American Flying Circus, at Vinton, Iowa, 1921

1

To Paris in two hours and twenty minutes

'WHAT would have been thought some fifty years ago', wrote Captain Bruce Ingram in September 1919, 'if anyone had seriously made the announcement that our business men would in a few years be able to have their lunch in London and their tea in Paris – that they would be able to work in the morning at their office, transact business in Paris, and return to London in time for dinner? And yet all this has now been rendered possible.'[1]

A few weeks earlier Captain Ingram had been a passenger on the recently inaugurated London–Paris service, pioneered by the Aircraft Travel and Transport Company. He travelled out to the aerodrome by District Railway to Hounslow station and then boarded a tram, which took him and his luggage to a not very convenient point just outside the aerodrome gates. 'This method of getting to the aerodrome, it is understood, has been or will be altered, and a motor-car service instituted, whereby passengers to Paris will be taken from a central place in London direct to the "departure platform".' There was, Captain Ingram felt, 'something incongruous' about reaching his aeroplane in this very slow and unremarkable way 'before being whirled through the air to France at a hundred miles an hour', and he is not the last person to notice the contrast.

After dealing with the Customs and passport authorities, and 'the usual impertinences of a declaration form', he walked to his aircraft, which was one of the Company's larger machines, 'containing four arm-chairs placed side-by-side in such a manner that, if you were sitting with your back to the engine, your neighbour faced the opposite way'. Before starting, the passenger compartment was 'roofed in by a sliding cover, with windows that could be opened or shut as desired, so that though all the passengers were in very close quarters, there was nevertheless no discomfort, and, above all, one could keep dry and warm whatever the weather'.

Departure was thirty-five minutes late, owing to the unpunctuality of one of Captain Ingram's fellow passengers, a Major-General. At 1 pm, however, the pilot, Major Patteson, M.C., D.F.C., 'who has made the journey to Paris and back some hundred and fifty times and who therefore knows the whole route as we know our back garden', took off and made for Paris. To begin with, the flight was comfortable enough, 'although there was enough wind to make it certain that many people travelling in the usual way[2] could not have had an enjoyable two hours, it is remarkable that all the way over the sea the aeroplane was perfectly steady'. Boulogne brought an unwelcome change. 'It was decidedly bumpy, and this bumping gives the feeling that one experiences when a lift suddenly descends and seems to leave part of one's anatomy behind. I gather that this "bumpiness" is not met with always, because Major Patteson – whose means of communicating with his four passengers was by passing written messages through a little "trap-door" in the partition behind his head, and who, in this way, kept up a running conversation with us – apologised for the uncomfortable movement of his machine. However, no one was disturbed.'

Two hours and twenty minutes after leaving Hounslow they were safely on the ground at Le Bourget, 'A car was waiting, and in a short twenty-five minutes more I was transacting the urgent business on which I had come, in an office in the middle of Paris.' The feelings of one passenger at least were ecstatic. 'One cannot hope to describe adequately the interest, the sense of security, and the comfort which such a journey gives to the passenger – to say nothing of the time saved, the avoidance of the inconveniences caused by the change from train to boat, and then from boat to train again, with the usual scramble for places, and the irritating delays at the Customs, experienced in the train and boat journey from London to Paris.'

The journey back was less peaceful. A heavy gale was blowing, 'not at all flying weather and the greatest discomfort was prophesied', but the pilot decided to leave and Captain Ingram found the return flight 'more varied and vastly more interesting than the other'. There was much to see and experience. 'At times it was found necessary to rise above the clouds, which were spread like a vast field of snow below us. At another time we entered a terrific squall, with driving rain – a magnificent and impressive sight.' Excitement and confidence seem to have prevailed over nervousness. 'At no time, whether in squall or cloud, was it possible to feel uneasiness – such a sense of security is given by these reliable machines and fine pilots of the Aircraft Travel Co.; machines and pilots that are regularly employed to take over members of the Cabinet and other important men during the sitting of the Peace Conference.'

'There is little doubt', Captain Ingram concluded, after trying it all for himself, 'that many will be tempted to make use of this service as passengers for the transaction of business where time is of vital importance; others will wish to cross over to Paris by air for the sake of the experience.' Even so, passengers did well to remember that the service was not really planned for them at all. 'The primary object is that of conveying important parcels and urgent communications which can reach their destination even more speedily than a telegram, and at a much cheaper rate.'

The 'members of the Cabinet and other important men' who flew regularly between London and Paris during the early months of 1919 included Bonar Law, Winston Churchill, Lord Milner and W. M. Hughes, the Prime Minister of Australia. They were carried in D.H.4As, single-engined biplanes operated by an RAF squadron specially formed for the purpose in March 1919. A daily courier and mail service was available in each direction. When the squadron was disbanded in September 1919, the aircraft were sold to Handley Page Ltd, along with hundreds of other surplus war machines.[3]

After the war, civil aviation was not permitted in Britain until April 1919. A Civil Aviation Department of the Air Ministry had been set up in February of the same year and an Air Navigation Act was passed shortly afterwards. This gave the Secretary for Air, acting through the Civil Aviation Department, powers to draw up air-traffic regulations. The first air-worthiness and registration requirements – the first not only in Britain but in the world – were issued on 30 April 1919, and civil flying was permitted from that date.

The first passengers to take advantage of the new possibilities were not the few dozens a week who wanted to fly to the Continent, but the thousands who were prepared to pay for a brief trip over and around the airfield – the joy-riders. C. G. Grey, the editor of *The Aeroplane*, had given his opinion several years before that commercial aviation would grow out of joy-riding. His calculations had been

. . . that out of the total population of this country some two million people would want the experience of having been up in an aeroplane, that a number of these would want to try it a second time, and that a very large proportion of the total number would go on joy-riding as often as they had the opportunity or could afford it; so that ultimately one might reckon that there would be some five million joy-rides to be given before the pleasure-flying market began to decline.[4]

What happened in 1919 was very encouraging to Mr Grey. A number of ex-RAF pilots, with no other congenial job to turn to, acquired old planes, mostly Avro 504K wooden trainers, which would otherwise have been scrapped, and set up in business to give their air-hungry fellow citizens a taste of flying, at a guinea a time.[5] One of the largest and most successful enterprises of this kind was at Blackpool, where Major Gordon McMinnies and his four pilots carried 10,000 passengers during June and July. Each pilot and machine made 42 trips in a ten-hour day, and still failed to clear the queues of people waiting to go up.

When the machines first started people were rather chary about trusting themselves into these strange-looking vehicles, having read so much about the heroism of aviators and the perils of aviation in the Press; but as the machines continued to operate day after day without an accident, and not only made the usual circular trips of a few minutes' duration round Blackpool, but actually flew regularly on a daily service between Blackpool and Manchester, the people began to realise that flying was nothing like as dangerous as they thought it was. There was just a sufficient spice of danger about it to make people brag about their flying experiences, and yet it was obviously safe enough for anybody to take the risk for the sake of saying they had flown.[6]

There can be no doubt that, in all countries where there was a supply of war-time pilots and planes, joy-riding did a great deal to prepare the public for scheduled services. Its main service, perhaps, was to convey the idea that flying was basically safe, since during the war the emphasis of newspapers and magazines had always been on the perils of flying and on the heroism of the men who flew. There was a certain irony in the situation, however, since the great majority of the joy-riders belonged to the lower-income groups while the early passengers on scheduled flights and charters came from much further up the social scale. The workers, in other words, proved that flying was safe, and enjoyed themselves in the process.

Punch, always critical of anything new, looked with small favour at the post-war fashion for flying. In August 1919 the magazine's house-poet turned his attention to joy-riding:

> Stranded at Brighton and bored to monotony,
> Sadly I roamed by the crowd-haunted shore;
> Fed up with bathing and boating and botany,
> Languidly humming the strains of 'Asthore';
> Then, in the offing, descended an aeroplane
> Gaily the pilot came striding my way;
> 'Afternoon, Sir!', he exclaimed, 'Would you dare a plane
> Voyage today?'
>
> Turning, I gazed with an eye that was critical
> At the contraption of fabric and wires;
> Flying's a game which my friends in the City call
> Simply gilt-edged – it uplifts and inspires.
> Holiday-makers stood by in expectancy
> Cinema merchants rushed up with their reels;
> 'Go it!' cried somebody, 'go an' get wrecked an' see
> Just how it feels.'
>
> I who had fought for a seat in an omnibus
> Surely could never recoil from a plane?
> There, newly painted, she stood like a Romney 'bus
> Bidding me soar through the vasty inane.
> Breathing a prayer for myself and my Fatherland
> Swiftly I scrambled aboard (the First Act)
> Upward we soared till I felt I would rather land
> Promptly – intact.

Swift rushed the air and the engine was thunderous;
'Say, shall I stunt you?' the pilot then roared.
Clouds were above us and Brighton was under us;
Peace reigned below – there was panic on board.
Fiercely pulsated by turbulent heart inside,
Fiercely we skidded and stunted and swayed;
Grimly I crouched in that brute of a Martinsyde
Dazed and dismayed.

Every mad moment seemed in its intensity
More than a cycle of slow moving years
Finally I, in a state of dumb density
Reached terra firma mid hurricane cheers.
Since I've decided that nothing can justify
Passenger flights in a nerve-racking 'plane;
Others may welcome a sport, but I'm cussed if I
Try it again.

The joy-riding companies themselves were more sensitive to the public mood, in which romance and a feeling of adventure and daring were about equally mixed. An interesting clue to this is a printed card, given to joy-riders in 1919 by Handley

2 Bringing flying to the people. Onlookers and passengers with Cobham's joy-riding plane at Reading, 1919

Page. The Handley Page crest is on the top left-hand corner of the first fold. Inside, the left-hand page shows a photograph of an aeroplane wing, with clouds below. At the top of the picture are the words 'Above the Clouds', and underneath (quoting Cowper)

> Regions Caesar never knew
> Thy posterity shall sway

To the right of the fold is

> A memento of a flight in a Handley Page
> aeroplane at Cricklewood Aerodrome on
> . . . .

The passenger or, if he was not too busy, the pilot, wrote the date in the space provided. The joy-rider was more than halfway to becoming a convert to air travel and, very important to the far from wealthy aviation industry, he had paid for his own conversion. It is difficult to think of a more economical form of advertising or public relations than joy-riding.

The outstanding British figure in this field was Alan (later Sir Alan) Cobham. Cobham's Flying Circus became famous during the 'twenties, with its displays of flying and a chance to take a trip up for oneself, from such places as Mumbles beach, near Swansea, for as little as 25p (5s.).

Flying outside Britain was not permitted until 14 July 1919. A commercial London–Paris flight, run by Air Transport and Travel Ltd, took place on the following day. This company was a subsidiary of the Aircraft Manufacturing Co., usually known as Airco. It had been formed in 1916 by George Holt Thomas, to run scheduled air services as soon as peace returned. Thomas's Aircraft Manufacturing Company, the predecessor of De Havilland, became the largest firm in the British aircraft industry. In 1919 it bought and converted surplus RAF planes, and Air Transport and Travel operated them. One board of directors controlled both companies. It included George Holt Thomas as Chairman, General Sefton Brancker as Managing Director, General Festing as Commercial Director and Captain Donald Grey as General Manager. Airco's chief pilot was Captain H. ('Jerry') Shaw who is still very vigorously alive. Captain Shaw first flew, as a passenger, on a joy-ride flight from Manchester racecourse in 1912. This was in a Blériot monoplane. After qualifying as a pilot during the winter of 1915–16, he went to France, 'where I flew everything'.[7] After the war he spent a period flying VIPs from Hendon to the Peace Conference. He left the RAF in a hurry, in order to avoid a court-martial as a result of cutting-in tactics calculated to annoy General Ludlow-Hewlett, who was trying to land at Kenley.

3 Joy-riding in 1919.
Alan, now Sir Alan, Cobham,
with two passengers at Reading

On 14 July 1919, Major Pilkington, of the St Helens glass firm, noticed a small paragraph in the London *Evening News*, saying that commercial air services between Britain and the Continent were at last permitted. He telephoned Airco at Hendon immediately, telling the company that he had an important meeting to attend in Paris on the following day and that he had missed the boat-train. He could keep his appointment only by flying. Airco agreed to take him from Hounslow, the only place where Customs facilities were provided, at 7.30 the next morning, and charged him £50 for the single journey. The aircraft was an Airco D.H.9, a converted civil version of the RAF D.H.9 light bomber. Both the pilot and the passenger sat in open cockpits. The weather on 15 July was bad. 'My log book records that there were low clouds and rain the whole way,' Captain Shaw recalled. 'When we reached the line of hills near Beauvais, the clouds were right down on the ground and we spent twenty minutes flying up and down before finding a break to get through. We took 2 hours 45 minutes for the whole flight, in spite of the wasted time, and that was slow in those days. Not bad when you remember that 12 years later Imperial Airways liners were scheduled to take 2 hours 30 minutes.'[8] Major Pilkington returned to London the next day, highly satisfied. After the scheduled daily service had begun on 25 August, he became a regular customer.

The inaugural Hounslow–Paris flight on 25 August carried one passenger (a Mr Stevenson-Race), newspapers, jars of Devonshire cream, several brace of grouse and a consignment of leather. In the first week there were twenty passengers. Two of them, an American and an Irish priest, returned from Paris on 28 August in 1 hour 45 minutes, with the help of a 100-mph hurricane. The pilot was Captain Shaw, and when they landed in England his passengers, who drank a bottle of brandy between Paris and London, told him they thought the unusual amount of movement during the flight had been caused by stunt-flying. 'The American's bowler hat had completely disintegrated; its brim was wedged around his chin, and damage to the cabin roof bore witness to the strength of his skull. The pilot's

4 De Havilland 4A converted bomber, similar to the one that opened the world's first international scheduled air service, Hounslow–Le Bourget, 25 August 1919

knuckles were raw where his hands had been smacking against the sides of the cockpit. The machine itself had to be completely re-rigged.'[9]

Aircraft Transport and Travel acquired two Continental associates, the Compagnie Général Trans-Aérienne, which operated single-seaters and carried only mail, and KLM, who, on 17 May 1920, opened a joint London–Amsterdam service with the British company. At that time KLM had no suitable aircraft of its own and rented them from Airco. Of the passengers on both the London–Paris and London–Amsterdam services 25 per cent. were, as Captain Shaw remembers them, business men. They included a mysterious Mr Weinberg, who went to Paris every Thursday. The remainder were 'Americans or holiday-makers', with a men/women ratio of about four to one. Children were very rare as passengers. One particularly good American customer was a Mr Simpson of Marshall Field. One evening Simpson received a message in Paris in the evening, saying that his wife had been taken ill in London. Shaw agreed to take him back on a charter flight the next morning, despite the bad weather. They were, however, compelled to land near Beauvais and to wait there until conditions improved, with Shaw paying no attention to Simpson's protests. In the early days, passengers of the 'I've-bought-the-plane-haven't-I?' type were not infrequent, especially on charter flights. They had to be told firmly that the pilot was in complete control, no matter how much the passenger might have paid for his ticket or how large a bribe he was offering. On the other hand, some part of a pilot's reputation was made by his ability to take off and land under conditions which grounded less skilful and less daring men.[10] There was certainly a financial incentive to fly whenever possible, because a pilot received extra money when he was actually in the air. Shaw, for instance, had £700 a year while he was with Air Transport and Travel, together with 50p (10s.) an hour flying pay.

Insurance for aircraft was certainly available in 1908,[11] and possibly earlier. To begin with, cover was provided only against fire, since the early aeroplane engines were very liable to burst into flames. Third-party cover was being widely sought by 1911, partly because most flying at that time was at exhibitions and meetings, where there was considerable danger to spectators, and partly because aeroplanes not infrequently had to land in unexpected places, with a consequent risk of damage to property, especially to crops and livestock. Animals were liable to stampede when an aeroplane was flying overhead and this resulted in many claims against pilots.

After 1918 the establishment of regular passenger flights brought about far-reaching changes in the aviation insurance market. Companies had to provide for the insurance of more expensive aircraft and for heavier personal accident losses. By the early 1920s, however, it had become common, if not normal, to include passenger coverage in the terms of the policy. An endorsement to a policy issued in 1922 agreed to 'cover all passengers carried by Messrs. Daimler Hire Ltd, against

5 Lignes Farman: cheque in payment for a flight on
the first civilian Paris–London flight, 18 January 1919

Legal Liability to Passengers as per Section 1 of the attached policy, limited to £1,000 any one passenger, excess £5 each & every claim, at a premium of 3/6 per passenger per flight, all passengers to be declared'. For some years there seems to have been no demand by airlines to insure against their liabilities to passengers on scheduled flights. Passengers consequently spent a good deal of money on insuring themselves. The people using air transport were generally well-to-do and therefore wished to insure themselves for fairly large sums, usually between £5,000 and £10,000, but sometimes as much as £100,000 or more. The rate for a passenger travelling between London and the Continent was £1 a thousand, roughly ten times the present rate.

In order to protect themselves against unreasonable losses, a number of insurers grouped together in 1920 to set up Lloyd's Aviation Record, on similar lines to Lloyd's Register of Shipping. This provided for a register of aircraft and pilots and for a worldwide system of aircraft surveyors. The surveyors were required to

inspect and classify aircraft, provide reports on aerodromes and routes and in-
vestigate accidents. It is interesting to notice that flying over sea was regarded as
particularly hazardous and in the early 1920s policies were often endorsed to the
effect that the shortest sea-crossings between Britain and France were to be undertaken, irrespective of the final destination. Night flying by scheduled airlines also
became subject to special consideration by underwriters, with additional premiums
being charged, the amount of which depended on the pilots and the routes taken.

Contrary to popular legend, the aircraft never at any time carried parachutes,
either for the pilot or his passengers. Few of the latter showed any signs of fear. The
company's explanation of this was a simple one: 'If you were frightened of flying,
you didn't fly. You went by train and boat.'

From the beginning, pilots were well treated in the matter of accommodation
and expenses. They were mostly put up in hotels, good hotels, but in Paris KLM
provided what Captain Shaw remembers as 'a sumptuous flat, with a resident
housekeeper'.

Throughout its short existence – it went out of business at the end of 1920 –
Aircraft Transport and Travel used only De Havilland aircraft. The original fleet
consisted of six D.H.4As and six D.H.9Cs. The D.H.9C conversion provided for
one passenger in front of the pilot and another behind him. In the opinion of the
pilot,

. . . there was nothing to choose between these two passengers' seats, because they were
both extremely uncomfortable. Each necessitated the use of Sidcot suits, flying helmets
and goggles – use of which was included in the fare of 20 guineas single. Only a contor-
tionist could get into the front seat, and once there he could not move, whilst the com-
parative roominess of the back seat was offset by the gale of wind rushing around the
whole time.[12]

The D.H.4A, which accommodated two passengers sitting face-to-face, was closed
in and rather more comfortable, but the first really commercial aircraft was Airco's
D.H.16, introduced on 8 September 1919. There was a four-seat cabin, with the
passengers facing one another in pairs. The D.H.18, which came into service in
March 1920, was an eight-passenger cabin machine, with the pilot placed behind
the passenger cabin.

In November 1919, Mary Hayman,[13] then a schoolgirl of fifteen, flew with her
father from the Handley Page aerodrome at Cricklewood to Brussels. They were
met at King's Cross and taken to Cricklewood in a chauffeur-driven car. At the
aerodrome they waited in a hut with two other passengers and were eventually told
there would be a delay, owing to fog. Three-quarters of an hour later the other
passengers had left to catch the boat-train, but Mrs Hayman's father was determined to fly – he liked anything new and was the sort of person to try flying as

soon as he could. When it was eventually decided that they should go, the pilot showed them the route on a map. They were to follow the railway lines to the coast and then take the shortest route across the Channel to Calais. Inside the plane were four wicker seats. On the two unused chairs there were piles of mailbags.

The return flight, the following May, was more eventful. As the plane flew over France it met strong headwinds and the pilot decided to land in a field. As they touched down, the plane tipped on one side. Nobody was hurt, but Mrs Hayman twisted her knee climbing out. They were approached almost immediately by a French policeman on a bicycle. His first words to them were 'May I see your papers?' The pilot had papers authorising him to land in France, but Mrs Hayman had a visa only for Belgium. On seeing this the policeman told her, 'You have no business to land here. You must leave as soon as possible.'[14] Fortunately the plane was undamaged. The farmer was paid to help them to right it and the remainder of the journey to London was uneventful.

The early passengers expected and received very little in the way of comfort or amenities. On the London–Paris service, after the first few months, they were taken from city-centre to city-centre. They registered at the office of the company, or of an agent, and were then driven to the aerodrome in a hire-car. Luggage was carried to and from the aircraft by mechanics, whom it was forbidden to tip. There was a 40 lb weight-limit for baggage, but it was not strictly enforced. The habit of weighing the passengers themselves was introduced during the mid-1920s.[15] The weighing machine at the office counter had its face politely turned inwards, so that only the clerk on duty could see it. The maximum weight allowance was for a passenger and his baggage together, so that a small, thin man could take a lot more luggage than a large, fat man. The name of one's next-of-kin was included with the facts about one's weight. The distribution of weight in the plane was almost as important as the total weight itself. If weather conditions were difficult, the airport authorities would work out the plane's centre of gravity and ask some of the passengers to move to other seats during take-off. The pilot shepherded his own passengers through the Customs on arrival and he was personally responsible for them until they and their baggage had been cleared.

There were no refreshment facilities at Hounslow, but this airfield was used only until 1 April 1920. Croydon, which then became London's civil airport, had a hotel, which had been an RAF mess, and a restaurant of sorts. Le Bourget and Amsterdam both had restaurants which were used mainly by visitors, not passengers, and did good business.

Until 1921 no reliable metereological information was available. Pilots had to trust their own experience and judgement. Broadly speaking, the only way of discovering what the weather ahead was like was to take off and find out. During

6 Air Union: the French actress, Mistinguett, disembarking from
a Farman 'Goliath' after making a London–Paris flight, 1923

1920 weather forecasts began to appear on the notice board at Le Bourget, but they
were of a type which pilots found it difficult to take very seriously. Expressions like
'bolsons in the Channel' and 'squaggy around Beauvais' appeared at intervals and
at the end of one bulletin was a note saying, 'The cloud height given in yesterday's
forecast as 3,000 metres should read 300 feet.'[16]

Air Travel and Transport soon ran into difficulties, as a result of inadequate
capital, insufficient passengers, especially for charters, and unsuitable planes. No
government support was forthcoming and the company closed down at the end of
1920.

It is interesting to notice, in view of later developments, the conditions for a
successful London–Paris service which were put forward by George Holt Thomas

in the paper 'Commercial Aeronautics', which he read to the Royal Aeronautical Society on 30 May 1918. In his opinion this route could be run profitably, at a single fare of £5 and with a 75 per cent. loading, if there were 40 passengers a day in each direction. Thomas, however, assumed the availability of 12-passenger aircraft, which his own company never in fact had. Using 12-seater planes, he estimated the total operating cost per seat-mile at 3 (old) pence, but the actual cost of running the 2- and 4-seater De Havillands, which were all Air Transport and Travel could get, ranged from 23 to 36 (old) pence. The fares charged therefore had to be very high and the traffic potential was correspondingly reduced.

In February 1921, a short time after Air Transport and Travel vanished from the scene, the other two British companies with international interests, Handley Page and Instone, were also compelled to withdraw their Continental services. The French, Dutch, Belgian and German governments were more realistic and saw from the beginning that civil aviation was going to need official nursing through its early stages. Subsidies of one kind and another were seen as worthwhile investments, which would later produce dividends in the form of increased national prestige, encouragement to aircraft manufacturers and commercial convenience.

In March 1921 the British government gave way to pressure and common sense and announced a small subsidy to Handley Page and Instone, who restarted their Paris service immediately. In 1922 they were joined by a third company, Daimler Airlines. The first effect of this was to produce over-capacity on the London–Paris route, with five companies, two French and three British, chasing a total volume of traffic which was as yet too small to allow any of them to make an adequate profit.

In September 1922 the British operators agreed to specialise: Instone taking London–Brussels, Daimler London–Amsterdam and Handley Page, which had the largest aircraft, London–Paris. The three Handley Page twelve-seaters, *Princess Mary*, *Prince George* and *Prince Henry*, went into service during the early summer of 1922. Handley Page made great efforts to promote these new aeroplanes and to persuade those who had not yet tried air travel that a pleasant new experience

7 Paris–London in the early 'twenties: Mrs Caroline Rogers, of North Andover, Massachusetts

awaited them. The approach, presented in a Handley Page booklet of 1922, was, 'Once you have flown to Paris, you will never go by boat again'.

Before the war, the hardier type of traveller went from London to Paris through the night, arriving at about 5 a.m. in an (at that hour) anything but gay city. It took a few hours to recover from the journey. Nowadays, unless you spend a night and half a day on the move from Waterloo, through Southampton–Havre you must at any rate use up nearly all the daylight hours. You must start after a very early breakfast, make sure of securing a seat, change from train to boat and from boat to train with incessant distraction of Passport and Customs formalities, and, thoroughly bored and weary, arrive in Paris in time for dinner. Your day has been spoilt, and your evening is ruined.

It stands to reason that a means by which you gain a useful morning in London, and arrive unjaded in Paris rather early for afternoon tea, in time, may be, to pay an important business call, or with leisure to do a little sightseeing before dinner, is worthy of some consideration. And especially if by this means you are saved from the confusion and irritation of changing from railway to steamer and back again, and are given, instead of a dull and uncomfortable railway journey with only an hour on the water (and that a torture to many) a glorious panorama of England and France, a short journey by motor-car at each end, and a beautifully simple and peaceful Customs office to go through, you will be wise to choose it. If your object be business it will save you valuable time, and probably a night's hotel expenses; if your object be pleasure you achieve it from the very start.'

Take the word of one who has tried and who knows. I first used the regular London–Paris air line because some little experience of air travelling, extending over many years, led me to look for just what I, in fact, found. And, be it said, not a few of those who travel to and from the Continent by air are those who having tried it once will never again, unless compelled to, go back to the railway and the boat.

Let me try to describe one trip. Not much of a morning (it so often is not in London!) as we hand ourselves and our suitcases to Handley Page Transport Ltd, presented in the person of the chauffeur who is to drive us to Cricklewood. The special Aviation section which is now a part of the daily weather forecast published in the daily newspapers speaks of 'much cloud' and only 'fair visibility'. On reaching the aerodrome we can see enough of the sky – not merely a thin street line of it – to judge. There is a haze, undoubtedly, and the trees at the far end of the big field are merely dim smudges. But we notice that the two propellers of one of the several machines standing about are steadily turning, and that two or three mechanics are hard at work there. Also we observe that on no face is there any anxiety or doubt; the start which we had for a few moments thought might possibly be delayed, or even prevented, is to be according to timetable. We venture to ask an official of the company, and he courteously assures us: 'Oh, this is all right. It is quite a good day. You will find it much clearer when you are out of London. And with no more wind than this it should be quite a quick crossing.'

Passports examined, we approach the machine, the propellers of which are still rotating – 'Just ticking over', we learn is the way of it. And then we step up the neat little steel ladder and enter the cabin, an attendant indicating a place. This is a comfortable wicker chair by an ample window. Already four other passengers are in their seats and three others soon follow. At the forward end of the cabin, we observe a door which communicates with the pilot's 'office'; and at the opposite end, close to the passenger's entrance, is another door, with the inscription 'Lavatory'. There is room to walk up the gangway between the two rows of seats. At each window are curtains. At intervals, transversely, there are diagonal cross-stays of stout steel tube.

The British may have pioneered in-flight lavatories, although KLM certainly ran them very close in this, but the credit for introducing in-flight meals should probably go to the French. By the mid-1920s their cross-Channel lunches had become splendidly elaborate affairs. A menu card of 1927 for Air Union's Paris–London service offered:

Servi à bord de l'Avion 'Capitaine Ferber'

Hors d'œuvre
Langouste Parisienne
Poulet Sauté Chasseur
Jambon d'York à la Gelée
Salade Niçoise
Glace Plombière
Fromages
Corbeille de Fruits

Paris, le 8 juillet 1927

The list of drinks included champagne, red and white Bordeaux, whisky, mineral waters and black coffee.

By 1924, when the British airlines were merged to form a single national airline, Imperial Airways,[17] the European and North African network of routes had expanded to a point where international timetables were being published. This was a French venture, the series being called *Guides des Voyages Aériens*. Each of the four booklets was of about sixty pages. The timetables centred on Paris, Paris–London; Paris–Brussels–Amsterdam; Paris–Lausanne–Geneva; and Paris–Prague–Warsaw. The London–Paris timetable has two quite different introductions: one is in English and the other in French. The English version, by Sir Sefton Brancker, is in the style of the Chairman's annual report to shareholders:

Today we have at our disposal five years of experience in the operation of the air route between London and Paris . . . As a result we have proved that Air Transport is a really safe means of travelling and that it saves much valuable time, even on so short a route as that between London and Paris, combined with a very high standard of comfort.
  The London to Paris route presents weather conditions which are peculiarly difficult for the operation of aircraft, but in spite of these difficulties, French and British pilots have maintained a very high measure of regularity, even during the worst season . . .

The French version, by Laurent Eynac, is much more enthusiastic and shows a

8 The Bréguet London–Paris service. Early 'twenties

fine poetic verve. The splendid original will be found below in the notes.[18] In translation it reads:

As Suares has written, the traveller is the most important element of the journey. Transports Aériens have made great strides during the past five years and have always taken pains to give their passengers safety, comfort, elegant décor, and the incalculable benefit of speed, of the opportunity to gain time, which is such a precious commodity in today's world.

Life expands in an aeroplane. The traveller is a mere slave in a train, and, should he manage to escape from this particular yoke, the car and the ship present him with only limited horizons. Air travel, on the other hand, makes it possible for him to enjoy 'the solitary deserts of infinite space'. It allows him to look around him freely and at never-ending variety. The earth speeds by below him, with nothing hidden and full of surprises, with its clear waters, its peaceful forests, its patient roads, its welcoming villages and fields.

At Le Bourget, introduce yourself to your pilot, who is always a man of the world and a war-time flying ace. He will shake you by the hand and give you a brief idea of what the flight will be like.

The London–Paris route taught the airline operators a number of useful and well-publicised lessons. The first and most important was that there was a market

28

for regular, dependable services among people to whom time mattered and that such people were prepared to pay a good deal in order to avoid the tedium and unpleasantness of a long train and boat journey, with all the changing, waiting, carrying and contact with officials this involved. The second discovery was that, in running an airline, economics counted quite as much as enthusiasm. Large aircraft, able to carry at least twelve passengers, were essential if fares were to be kept down to a figure which would allow the market to expand. Even with suitable aircraft, however, a government subsidy was essential and some means had to be found of planning services so that there were not too many operators chasing too little traffic and going bankrupt in the process.

A government contract to carry mail often allowed a company to run a passenger service as well, on a basis of letters subsidising people. Such a service could provide remarkably good value, although passengers had to remember that their needs and convenience came second to those of the postal authorities. In 1927, for example, it was possible to travel from London to Ireland by air. The Royal Mail plane was boarded at North Weald aerodrome and the flight was then via Renfrew, to pick up the Scottish mail, and Belfast. The five-hour journey cost only 10p (2s.) more than the normal train and boat crossings, but only four passengers could be taken on each flight and there was considerable competition for seats.

The coming of larger and more comfortable aircraft did not, however, mean the end of flying's adventurous days. One of Imperial Airways' secretarial staff at Croydon[19] between 1926 and 1929 recalls a number of unpublished facts from this period, at a time when the public was being assured daily that flying was as safe as travelling by train.

Once, when she was acting as a relief telephonist, she heard a distress call from a pilot over the Channel: 'I am coming down in the ditch.' He landed in the sea seven miles north-west of the Varne lightship, with a dozen passengers on board, including women and children, and a Pekingese dog. They managed to get out of the plane and sat on the wings, waiting to be picked up. They all remained calm,

9 A mishap in Roumania. Paris–Bucharest flight, 1924

Granddaughter. "DON'T YOU WISH YOU WERE GOING BACK BY AEROPLANE, GRANNIE?"

Grannie. "NO, MY DEAR, CERTAINLY NOT. I DON'T HOLD WITH THEM. I ALWAYS KEEP TO THE GOOD OLD-FASHIONED RAILWAYS, AS NATURE INTENDED US TO, MY DEAR."

10 The Generation Gap. *Punch*, 14 August 1929

except for a Greek, who, as soon as he saw the lifeboat was approaching, took off his boots, dived into the sea and started swimming towards the boat, determined at all costs to be saved. To the delight of all the other passengers, the lifeboat circled round him, collected all the other passengers first, and then picked him up on the way back. He later sued the company for the loss of his boots.

From about 1925, civil flying followed two quite different patterns. In the industrialised, prosperous parts of the world the task was to persuade the people who normally travelled by rail and sea to transfer their patronage to the airlines. Elsewhere, as in South America, Australia and much of Africa, the problem was to run air services of a very basic kind, which would move people quickly across areas of difficult country, where no transport facilities previously existed. Those who were railway travellers – mainly first-class passengers – demanded a standard of comfort which compared with that of a Pullman coach. The people of Brazil, Russian Central Asia and the Congo were grateful for anything better than a horse or a small river-boat.

America was a slow starter in the aviation business. Her first scheduled passenger services date only from 1926, although much experience had been gained with transporting mail before that, but thereafter progress was extremely rapid, mainly because of the great and obvious advantages which air travel brought to industry and commerce. In the United States, during the late 1920s and early 1930s, there was community pressure to get airports established, to an extent that did not occur in any other country. Much of the credit for this must be given to a well-organised pressure-group, the National Aeronautics Association of the U.S.A., which set up local 'chapters' to get things moving. 'It should be the aim of every Chapter', said the Association, 'to obtain improved landing and supply facilities for airplanes and airships in the community, and to encourage inter-city flying as a business enterprise.'[20] The results of this campaign were very impressive. In 1935 an Irish visitor to the United States noted

. . . the matter-of-fact way in which the general public, whether they fly or not, regard airlines. There is none of the attitude of looking upon flying as a 'stunt' which obtains, even in European countries which are quite advanced in air transport, amongst those who have not actually flown. America has reached the stage of taking flying for granted as part of the normal transportation machinery of the nation.[21]

11 What potential passengers were used to. Pullman-car
comfort on the London, Midland and Scottish Railway, 1928

12 Travel luxury on the Continent. The 'Rheingold Express', 1928. The major airlines
aimed at providing a degree of spaciousness and comfort comparable with rail-travel

2

The early years of comfort and snobbery

THE DEVELOPMENT of civil aviation during the 1920s and 1930s owed a great deal to the Dutch and particularly to the extraordinary drive and single-mindedness of KLM's founder, Albert Plesman. Plesman established KLM in October 1919, with three priorities quite clear in his mind. He needed adequate capital, aeroplanes specially designed to carry passengers, and an air-minded public. Given these, he had no doubts about succeeding.

In August and September 1919, Plesman organised an aviation exhibition in Amsterdam. Half a million people visited it and 4,000 of them paid 40 guilders each for a flight. Largely as a result of the publicity from this exhibition, Royal Dutch Airlines (KLM) was founded the following month as a limited company with a reasonable capital and valuable support from the banks and other commercial institutions. While it was waiting for new aircraft to be designed and manufactured, KLM gathered experience by hiring crews and planes from other operators, including, as mentioned in the previous chapter, the British company, Aircraft Transport and Travel. On the Amsterdam–London service, inaugurated on 17 May 1920, the water-cooled engine and instruments (compass, air-speed indicator, tachometer and petrol gauge) were not considered safe for long journeys over water, so the flights were routed down the Dutch and Belgian coast and then up to London via Folkestone and Tonbridge. Another experimental service, from Amsterdam to Bremen and Hamburg, was started in September 1920, with aircraft and pilots from a German company, Deutsche Luftreederei.[1]

In April 1921 KLM opened regular services over these routes with its own crews and its own German-built[2] Fokker F.II monoplanes. These had a closed cabin for four or five passengers and were much more comfortable to travel in than the borrowed German planes. Three passengers sat on a bench seat and two in easy chairs. They cruised at 80 mph. The Fokker F.III, introduced in November of the same year, had a separate freight compartment, so that passengers, baggage and freight were no longer mixed together. The eight-seater Fokker F.VII, which entered service in 1924, included two important developments, plane-to-ground radio-telephony and a lavatory. An improved version of the F.VII, in service from

May 1925 onwards, had air-cooled radial engines, metal propellers, a heated cabin and sponge-rubber seating.

At this time an article called 'Six People Fly to Copenhagen' appeared in a new German aviation periodical, *Ikarus*.[3] The flight was from Tempelhof, Berlin, and the writer, Dr Heinz Orlovius, describes the group of passengers and makes certain deductions about them. One appears to be a businessman, thinking only about the timetable and whether the plane will be punctual. The second, a man with an artistic look about him, seems to be asking, 'Is the plane safe? What happens if we come down over the water? I must get there in time. My concert's at 8 o'clock.' It is extraordinary, says Dr Orlovius, to see how used the people at the airport seem to be to these sorts of questions. 'Everybody's questions are answered.' Another one of the party seems to be a farmer, and it doesn't need a Sherlock Holmes to know what he is going to Copenhagen for. There is a catalogue of a big cattle sale and show in Copenhagen sticking out of his pocket.

Numbers four and five are pretty easy to guess, too. They are a young couple with shiny new rings on their fingers, saying, 'It is wonderful to be Icarus and to know that the Sun God cannot destroy our wings, because our wings are made of aluminium.' The plane is safe and comfortable. Inside, Dr Orlovius remarks, 'there is nothing to distinguish your surroundings from those of a luxury express train', a comparison frequently made by every airline during the 'twenties and 'thirties.

Another German periodical[4] investigated the air-travel market in the same year that the observant Dr Orlovius flew from Berlin to Copenhagen. In its leading article it put the question 'Why not travel by air?' and supplied the most frequently heard answers. Air travel was commonly thought to be 'Uncomfortable. Dear. Dangerous.' The magazine denied all three criticisms. 'The objection that you buy saving of time and the romantic journey at the cost of danger to your own life', it declared, 'is an argument more appropriate to our grandfathers than to ourselves.' It then went on to give a list of what it called 'people suitable as passengers'. Air travel, it felt, was the most appropriate way of transporting 'exceptional business-men, clever tourists, romantic honeymoon couples, fast-moving directors, modern lawyers, anxious motorists, attractive mannequins, fresh oysters and crabs, expensive silks and perfumes, breakable electric bulbs and sensitive furs and chemicals'.

No European or American airline would have disagreed with this list of desirable passengers, and considerable ingenuity was devoted to securing as many of them as possible. The British and German companies became particularly good at the snob approach, never failing to draw public attention to the statesmen, titled people, film stars and millionaires who travelled on their aircraft and who had presumably found everything to their satisfaction. In 1927 Imperial Airways reported[5] that 'On June 20th, H.R.H. Prince George, who travelled incognito, made a trip from

13 Boarding the aircraft.
KLM in 1927

14 Grands Express Aériens. First commercial night-flight, Paris–London, 7 June 1922

15 Silver Wing to Paris. 'The standard by which aerial standards are set'. Late 'twenties

Paris to London; unlike H.R.H. the Prince of Wales, who flew from Paris to London last spring in a "Special", Prince George travelled by the regular "Paris Shopping Service".' Prince George seems to have enjoyed flying. A few weeks later it was reported that 'Imperial Airways have been honoured by H.R.H. Prince George travelling as a passenger on the Paris route. On this occasion he travelled in one of the aircraft operating the "Silver Wing" Service de Luxe.'[6] The Silver Wing Service was Imperial Airways' appeal to the élite. In 1931–32 their London–Paris service was in two parts: Service A was usually operated by the Argosy class of 3-engined 20-seater aeroplane and Service B, the Silver Wing, used Heracles 38-seaters. Service A cost £4 4s. single, £7 19s. 6d. return, and Service B £4 12s. 6d. single, £8 15s. return. These fares were about 50 per cent. higher than those charged for travel by sea and rail. Service A left Croydon at 8.30 am and Service B at 12.30 pm. Each had a flying time of 2¼ hours.

Air fares showed no tendency to fall during the 'twenties and early 'thirties, even though more passengers could be carried on each flight. In 1928 Imperial Airways charged, for example, £4 single to Amsterdam and £9 10s. to Berlin, with no reduction for a return ticket. By 1932 these rates had gone up to £5 and £10 respectively.

Royalty, no matter what their nationality, were invaluable to the airlines and their patronage rarely went unmentioned. In August 1927 Imperial Airways, who by this time were running services in the Middle East, noted that

... we had the distinction of carrying on the Cairo–Basra service H.M. King Feisal and the Emir Ghazi of Iraq. Earlier in the month, the heir to the throne of Iraq, who was returning from Harrow accompanied by his tutor, travelled in the 'City of Baghdad' between Cairo and Baghdad. H.M. King Feisal, attended by Tashin Bey Khadri and other members of his suite, flew from Baghdad to Gaza. During the flight the King sent out by wireless a message of brotherly greeting for the Emir Abdulla of Transjordania.[7]

This, however, was outdone by a later item,[8] from the same airline:

We shall in future publish each month a list of the most distinguished and interesting passengers who have travelled on our London–Paris services since the last issue. Below we give a list for the first three weeks in March:—

> Lord Londonderry, Secretary of State for Air
> Lady Carlisle
> Marqués Bonneval
> Prince and Princess Walkonsky
> Baron Rothschild
> Lord Lymington
> Count Spezia
> Baroness Doiney

16 Publicising air travel in the early nineteen-thirties.
The famous Fratellini clowns fly Lufthansa

Marquis Traeontal
Mr. Edward Marjoribanks, M.P. for Eastbourne
M. René Clair, French film producer
Mr. Eyston, Racing motorist
Mr. Kaye Don, Racing motorist
Mr. Jeff Dickson, Boxing promoter
Primo Carnera, Italian boxer

The implication was two-fold. On the one hand the ordinary citizen could be expected to feel that what was good enough for Prince George, Princess Walkonsky and Primo Carnera must be good enough for him, and, on the other, one Princess was reckoned to be attractive bait for another Princess.

The mention of Prince George and the Paris Shopping Service was a useful move. The appeal of this particular flight was bound to be considerably increased if it became known that the Royal Family might be going on the same trip. Imperial Airways' publicity department did not, of course, say this in as many words, but the mere hint had valuable commercial possibilities. It was very proud of its Paris Shopping Service, which left Croydon in the morning and returned in time for dinner. The month after Prince George occupied one of the twelve not-inexpensive seats, this note appeared:

On the arrival at Croydon recently of the regular afternoon Paris Shopping Service, it was noticed that the twelve passengers were all ladies. This is only another indication of the fascination that flying has for women, and the increasing popularity of the Paris Shopping Service. Doubtless the time is not far distant when one will see the same reservation of Aircraft for Ladies Only as is now made by Railway Companies for the convenience of women travellers.[9]

Film stars, Middle Eastern princes and visiting American senators may have provided the airlines with their glamour and box-office appeal, but, over the twelve months, businessmen were its bread and butter. In trying to win them over from the railways, the emphasis during the 1920s was always on speed, very rarely on comfort. In 1928 Imperial Airways drew attention to the enterprise of a party of American businessmen. Travelling in a fourteen-seater Handley Page airliner, they visited Paris, Cologne, Hanover, Berlin, Prague, Vienna, Budapest, Basel, and London, all in fourteen days, 'a trip impossible by any other form of transport'.[10]

Not only businessmen were attracted by the speed of air travel. One day during the summer of 1927,

Mr. S. Donoghue, the famous jockey, rode in the 2 o'clock race at Windsor, and in a race at 4.30 at Ostend on the same day. After the Windsor race he was rowed across the river to a meadow where a fast aeroplane awaited him. Although a stop was made at Croydon Aerodrome for Customs formalities, Mr. Donoghue reached Ostend at 3.45, where a motor-car was waiting to take him to the race course. He actually arrived at the race course with half an hour to spare.[11]

A similar case involved a London surgeon, 'who, having received an urgent summons, flew from Croydon to Le Touquet, and performed a successful operation two hours after leaving Croydon. Returning the following morning by air, he was able to keep appointments in his consulting rooms before mid-day.'[12] This type of traveller obtained speed and convenience by chartering a plane to meet his special needs. He bought personal service and paid a lot for it; a four-seater plane cost £25 a mile.

There were other ways of obtaining privileged treatment. On the London–Paris service there were early attempts to sort out the passengers into two classes, so that the famous and influential might have an opportunity to avoid the company of their social inferiors. The separation into sheep and goats could not be guaranteed, but by making some aeroplanes more expensive than others there was a good possibility of achieving the desired results, especially since the first-class services departed at more convenient times and used more up-to-date aircraft. There was always a risk, of course, that princesses might choose to travel second class, rather than first, if the alternative were open to them, but there were methods of discouraging them. Occasionally, however, these tactics produced unexpected results. Having patted themselves on the back by noting that 'the success of the introduction of second-class fares on the London–Paris service proves that air travel on this route is now accessible to many from whom it has hitherto been debarred', the Company went on to tell a moral tale.

It was pointed out to a lady who enquired recently for particulars of the second-class service that goods, and possibly dogs, would be carried on the second-class aeroplanes. Her reply that she 'just adored dogs' provided a booking clerk with a selling point which was certainly not in mind when the new service was planned.[13]

The airlines were faced with the always-difficult problem of trying to appeal to an élite and to everybody, at the same time. They had to say, on the one hand, 'Everyone flies nowadays', and, on the other, 'All the best people fly'. It was not an easy task and, forty years later, one can only marvel at how well they succeeded, at a time when public relations was still in its infancy.

Certain amenities were bound to commend themselves to all passengers, however. This was particularly true of arrangements at airports, which had been primitive to begin with, but improved rapidly, at least at the major centres, during the 1920s. There was no reason why a person travelling from Le Bourget or Croydon should be given poorer conditions than one using the Gare de Lyon or Victoria. An international airport was not a flying club, nor was it a war-time airfield, although the difference was not always appreciated, either by governments or by airline operators.

Le Bourget was very proud of the facilities it was offering by the mid-1920s.[14] Accommodation for passengers was on the first floor, 'where there is a very fine view over the airport'. There was a waiting room, *bureau de change*, post and telegraph office and a range of telephone kiosks. In addition, 'as at railway stations', there was a bookstall.

The new buildings at Croydon Airport, paid for by the Air Ministry, opened on 30 January 1928, 'when all services will start from the fine expanse of paving which takes the place of the "tarmac" of the old aerodrome. On entering the domed Booking Hall, one realises that air services have now taken their place in the civilised world as a recognised means of transport, no longer limited to a few adventurous spirits, but used daily by business men as well as those travelling for pleasure.'[15]

An English doctor, travelling from Croydon to Le Bourget on 18 September 1931, wrote down his experiences in great detail.[16] After checking in at the Air Union office at 52 Haymarket, where he was weighed and handed in his passport, Dr Stein and his fellow passengers walked out to the airport bus. 'A flower-seller

17 Basic passenger amenities in the early 'thirties.
Embarking in a Dornier 'Merkur', 'somewhere in Bavaria'

18 Looking after an élite. Passengers boarding a
'Heracles' London–Paris flight, c. 1931. The passenger-door
was low enough not to need steps

19 Ellen Church, the world's first airline stewardess (1930).
She is shown here wearing her original stewardess uniform
and standing in the doorway of a United Airlines DC-3

outside', he felt, 'was very importunate with her white heather – doubtless for the superstitious who wished to guard against crashing.' In the bus 'there were more than were travelling. I think if you are seeing someone off they take you there and back free.'

Once in the aircraft, 'I take a seat near the back, where the view is not obstructed by the wings; the engine is running, so I plug my ears with cotton wool. I look around me; there is a notice to say that no smoking is allowed, and the inevitable "It is forbidden to throw anything out of the window." The Imperial Airways machine also has "It is dangerous to open the door while the aeroplane is in motion." '

Conditions in the air are a little rough. 'Occasionally we bump; the sensation is something like the giant racer at Wembley and something like a boat in a rough sea.' It is, however, lunch-time. 'The man on my left is drinking whiskey and Schweppes and munching something. I call the steward and he brings me biscuits and cheese at three times their earthly prices, but, then, such things are to be expected in heaven.'

A French girl on a nearby seat is in no mood to eat or drink. 'The steward comes up to her and takes a brown paper bag away, in exchange for which he gives her another. Why does she hold it like a nose-bag? Ah, I see. It is marked

AIR UNION
Pour le mal de l'air.'

During the late 1920s the German airline, Deutsche Lufthansa, made outstanding contributions towards improving the comfort of travellers. The aeroplane which achieved this was the three-engined Junker's G-31, which took fifteen passengers. The seats could be made fully reclining for night journeys and there was a properly equipped galley, which earned the G-31 the name of the 'flying dining-car', and gave Lufthansa an opportunity to claim the distinction of being the first airline in the world to serve hot meals during flights[17] and the first to include a steward as a member of the crew. This pioneering steward was Albert Hofe, who had many years' railway experience with the Mitropa Company.

The first stewardesses, however, were American. Boeing Air Transport, which later became part of United Air Lines, were employing eight of them in May 1930. No other airline adopted this idea until 1933. The eight pioneers were all registered nurses. They wore white nurses' uniforms during a flight and green woollen twill suits, with capes and berets, on the ground. They earned 125 dollars a month for 100 hours' work. One of them, formerly Inez Keller and now Mrs Richard J. Fuite, has recalled her days as a stewardess.[18] She flew in Boeing 80As, taking a dozen passengers the 950 miles between Oakland and Cheyenne, Wyoming, with five stops. 'It was supposed to take eighteen hours, but it was usually more like

20 Christmas in the air, aboard an Imperial Airways Handley Page W. 10, 1928

21 c. 1937. Passengers and crew observe the Two Minutes
Silence on Armistice Day on an Imperial Airways Short L.17

twenty-four. If the weather got bad, we would land in a field for a while and wait for the storm to clear up.' The planes flew at a height of 2,000 feet. They were not heated, pressurised or air-conditioned. Mrs Fuite found the absence of pressurisation the most difficult to tolerate. 'One day, after I had been flying four months, I lost the hearing in my left ear when the plane hit an air pocket near Reno and dropped 500 feet. I quit a few days later, because I didn't want to go deaf in my other ear.'

The work of these stewardesses was a good deal more varied then than it is nowadays. 'We had to carry all the baggage on board,' Mrs Fuite remembers, 'and if the seats weren't fastened down tightly, we had to screw them down ourselves. Then we had to dust the whole plane. Some of us had to join bucket brigades to help fuel the airplanes. We also helped pilots push planes into hangars. And we had to make sure the passengers didn't open the exit door by mistake when they were going to the washroom.' If all the seats were full, the stewardess had to sit on a mailbag or a suitcase in the rear of the plane.

The food served was exactly the same any time of the day – coffee or tea, fruit cocktail, fried chicken and rolls. The planes had steam-chests to heat up the food and drink.

22 'Seven passengers, twelve bags'. A London–Paris passenger list, 1935

The passengers took to the new stewardesses very quickly, but the pilots were less enthusiastic. 'The pilots', Mrs Fuite remembers, 'didn't want us at all. They were rugged temperamental characters, who wore guns to protect the mail. They wouldn't even speak to us during the first couple of trips. The wives of the pilots weren't very excited about the idea, either. They began a letter-writing campaign to Boeing, saying that the stewardesses were trying to steal their husbands and requesting their removal. One pilot's wife in Salt Lake City always met her husband at the plane. She was really jealous.'

Gratitude, rather than jealousy, seems to have been the usual reaction of the passengers to this latest addition to the amenities provided by the airlines. One seasoned traveller[19] recalled that before the days of air hostesses he made a habit of saying this prayer before take-off: 'Please God, take me safely to where I'm going' (he would specify his destination), and on landing he always used to say, 'Thank you, sir.' After the introduction of hostesses, however, he no longer felt impelled to ask for divine protection. These uniformed young women filled him with confidence. If they were brave, then he should be, too.

The year before United made history with their stewardesses, Transcontinental Air Transport (TAT), a predecessor of Trans-World Airlines, established a coast-to-coast link across the United States in forty-eight hours. Night flying was still not practicable, so passengers travelled by night in rail-Pullman berths. Going East–West the stages were:

1. New York–Columbus, Ohio, by rail, on 'The Airway Limited'.
2. Columbus–Waynoka, Oklahoma, by air.
3. Waynoka to Clovis, New Mexico, by rail, on the Santa Fé's 'Missionary'.
4. Clovis to Los Angeles by air.

In November 1930 the transcontinental travel time was cut to thirty-six hours, with no rail travel. There were ten stops, with an overnight rest at Kansas City. By 1932, TWA had mastered night flying, eliminated the stop-over and cut the journey to twenty-four hours.

In 1932, Hudson Fysh, of Qantas, visited the United States for the first time and flew by night from Chicago to Los Angeles.

Our plane was full all the way and there were an Admiral and a 6 months old baby on board. What with the lighted way, experienced pilots, two way radio, and the route system of radio, it appeared quite safe to me, but I admit I would not have liked to cross the mountains in the weather we got about Iowa City. We were held up there by bad weather for 3 hours, a big thunder storm, and then went off into the tail end of it. There is a ground every 20 miles all lit up for landing and every 10 miles a revolving beacon – so that you can see it is hard to go wrong while there is any visibility at all. This organized route – costing in capital and operating cost Heaven knows what – is of course the only factor which makes this wonderful night passenger service possible.[20]

TAT were early advocates of safety belts. One of their passengers described[21] how this part of flight discipline worked. Having selected a seat number at the air terminal, he went aboard and fixed his 'light safety belt'. After they were airborne 'the courier comes down the aisle, smiling cheerfully, and tells us we can remove the belts and open the windows. The belts, he explains, are used more to keep the passengers in their seats during landings and takeoffs than for safety purposes. The windows are to be closed while on the ground to keep out cinders, mud or water.

'On his way back down the aisle the courier hands each of us a letter of welcome from TAT officials, a small folder containing facts regarding the plane and the line, a small oiled paper containing cotton for the ears, and a package of chewing gum.

On this trip, food was served after leaving St Louis. The steward, whom the passengers knew as 'Canfield', 'brings out light aluminium trays which are supported by brackets on the fuselage wall and a leg on the aisle so as to rest firmly in front of each passenger. He produces the box lunches, which are found to include chicken salad, cheese and egg salad sandwiches, a pickle, salt and sugar, coffee, cream, cake, and an apple and banana.'

In 1935 the Bureau of Air Commerce at the Department of Commerce produced some statistics to show that flying in the United States was getting safer each year.

During the fiscal year 1935, aircraft on scheduled services flew 5,807,933 miles for each fatal accident that occurred. From these figures, covering the period from 1st July, 1934, to 31st December, 1934, the experts draw the following conclusions. At 150 miles per hour a passenger could fly an average of 1,613 days (almost three and one-half years) continuously for twenty-four hours a day, before running the risk of being involved in a fatal accident.[22]

United Air Lines, said their Western Traffic Manager in 1935,[23] used four criteria for running their services – 'safety, speed, comfort and economy'. Comfort was to a large extent in the hands of their stewardesses, 'chosen for personality and character'. Each of these stewardesses, said United, was considered a very important member of the crew.

It is her pleasant duty to look after the needs of the travellers, to make them comfortable, to point out various scenic points of interest and to serve specially prepared meals. No effort or expense has been spared to obtain the very best of food for these meals. United recently signed a contract with a famous San Francisco hostelry to supply outgoing aircraft with de luxe meals. An unusual feature of this service is each lunch is kept cool and fresh by the use of dry ice, actually the first time that dry ice has been used aboard a commercial aircraft. The ice is so wrapped in cellophane that the food is never allowed to freeze, but simply ensures that the natural moisture and freshness of the food is retained.

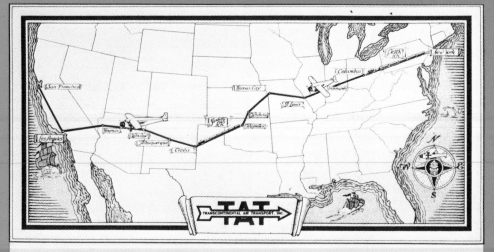

Officers of TRANSCONTINENTAL AIR TRANSPORT, Inc.

C. M. KEYS, *President*

PAUL HENDERSON
Executive Vice-President

CHARLES A. LINDBERGH
Chairman, Technical Committee

PAUL F. COLLINS
General Superintendent

J. V. MAGEE
Managing Vice-President

T. B. CLEMENT
General Traffic Manager

AMELIA EARHART
Ass't. to General Traffic Manager

23

24

The PENNSYLVANIA announces ·· 48 hour Coast to Coast Service by RAIL and AIR

Effective July 7th from New York
July 8th from Columbus and Los Angeles

"... the word 'Railroad' no longer is adequate to describe the transportation service which up-to-date railroads now offer to the public. We are no longer railroads alone; we are transportation companies.

"We must be prepared to offer our railroad service where it is most desirable, or bus service, or service by airplane. We must adjust our freight facilities more and more to the needs of the individual shippers. In other words, my view of a railroad is that it should give the people the kind of transportation they want ...

GENERAL W. W. ATTERBURY,
President of the Pennsylvania Railroad

"INAUGURATE service when everything is ready—not one minute before!"

A large staff of experts in many fields has worked for months with the idea of making

this new Rail-Air Service a solid and enduring foundation for developments of the future.

Air routes have been selected, mapped, tested by flights. Millions of dollars have been spent in the building of extensive airports. Emergency landing fields have been laid out at regular intervals along the carefully prepared routes. Airplanes have been most rigorously tested.

A private meteorological system has been worked out in conjunction with government and other agencies. Also an elaborate system of communication (teletype, radiophone, wireless) does unites airport with airport and airport with plane—so that planes en route are constantly receiving last-minute weather reports and other information.

In short, everything has been done to insure in this new enterprise the highest standards of efficiency, speed, safety.

The Night by Train—the Day by Plane

Suppose you are westbound from New York. You board The Airway Limited at 6:05 P. M. (Standard Time).

You sleep in this luxurious Pennsylvania train all night. Bright and early the next morning, at Port Columbus, you leave the train and take your seat in a Transcontinental Air Transport, Inc., plane.

From Port Columbus your flight is direct—with just enough stops to provide variety: Indianapolis, St. Louis, Kansas City, Wichita. An appetizing luncheon is served in the plane en route. At 6:24 P. M. you arrive at Waynoka, Oklahoma, where you transfer to a Santa Fe train.

At Clovis, New Mexico, the next morning you board another swift and luxurious plane—and that afternoon you are in Los Angeles; thence by plane next morning to San Francisco. Eastbound the journey is equally convenient by the same route, using the same facilities.

Soar like the Eagle! ... Swift and sure, these planes glide smoothly over the colorful patchwork of Middle West fields and farms, the majestic Mississippi, the mountains of Arizona, the picturesque towns of New Mexico—some of the most beautiful scenery in America.

Westbound, you begin your westward 48-hour journey in style on the Pennsylvania Flyer. The Airway Limited which takes you as far as Columbus. The The Airway Limited cars have the conveniences of a private dining car, observation car, club cars, shower bath, valet, the latest Pullman equipment, newspapers and magazines, stock quotations, baseball and football returns in course.

These planes accommodate comfortably ten passengers. There is adequate storage space for your hand baggage. All the interior arrangements are in perfect taste ... You might think you were in the observation car of The Airway Limited.

PENNSYLVANIA RAILROAD

Carries more passengers, hauls more freight than any other railroad in America

25 Coast to Coast: Mrs Howard Willett leaving Penn Central Station, New York

23 Coast to coast, by plane and train. The TAT route and officers, 1929

24 The TAT route. Standards of comfort

Usually these meals consist of such delicacies as chicken and fruit salads, cold meats, light sandwiches, cheeses, ice cream, pastries, etc. Hot coffee, cocoa, tea and soups are kept in large thermos bottles.

In America, United go on to state, it had already become uneconomic for businessmen to travel in any other way but by air.

Recently a statistician prepared the following figures which show that it is unprofitable for people making as much as $1 an hour to travel by surface transport, providing they reckon that their time is as valuable to the company as the company estimates it on the basis of the salary:

Traveller's Salary per hour	Bus	Total Cost Rail	Air
$0.40	$8.45	$11.27	$14.86
0.50	9.50	11.92	15.09
0.60	10.55	12.57	15.65
0.75	12.12	13.54	15.65
1.00	14.75	15.17	16.22
2.00	25.25	21.67	18.48
3.00	35.75	28.17	20.75
4.00	46.25	34.67	23.03

(These figures appear to be based on a journey occupying $1\frac{3}{4}$ hours by air and on the following relative speeds: aircraft 1.00; train 0.26; bus 0.16.)

When the air transport companies convince the men who direct industrial corporations that a man with a salary of $5,000, $10,000 to $30,000 a year is not as valuable to them when he uses surface transport as he is when he puts in his time working instead of travelling, air transport will experience an even more rapid growth than in the past. It is difficult to argue that the services of an employee are so valuable that he has to be paid a high salary if he takes four days to travel from coast to coast, when it is possible to travel without the loss of a single business hour from New York and many eastern cities to any major point on the Pacific Coast.

In Europe, the search for ways of providing greater comfort continued. For many years noise continued to be a serious problem. Imperial Airways made great play with the improvement to be found in the new and much praised Heracles class. The Heracles machines, made by Handley Page, were large, lumbering, comfortable and safe. One of them, piloted by Captain O. P. Jones, had the distinction of being the first British airliner to be struck by lightning. Captain Jones recalled that

The cockpit was walled with glass, like a conservatory, and when the lightning hit us it all blew out. There was even glass in the engines. I managed to get back to Croydon without mishap, but it was a very draughty trip home.[24]

Captain Jones had many other interesting experiences with this aircraft, more than one in connexion with night landings. For example,

The 'Heracles' had magnesium flares fitted under the wingtips which burnt, in a downward direction, for the final two minutes of the approach. On one occasion, coming into Le Bourget, they burnt in an upward direction and soon the wings were blazing away merrily. We had no passengers aboard at the time, and, after we came down to a beautifully illuminated landing, I got the crew out and taxied round in very fast circles until the fire-engines arrived.

'The double journey between London and Paris', it was reported of the Heracles service,[25] 'can now be accomplished in a day with no more fatigue than used to be caused by the single trip. The difference consists mainly in the reduction of engine noise and vibration, in the big new airliners of Imperial Airways, to a degree about equal to that of an express train.' Even so, the magazine *Aviation* felt able to write, a few months later,

. . . when everything possible has been said of fear and fare, alternative twins, between which the blame for unsatisfactory traffic returns has always been distributed, there

26 The restaurant at Schipol Airport, Amsterdam. Late 'twenties

remain other factors that keep people off the airlines and account for some cases of implacable hostility on the part of former passengers. Foremost among them is noise. We feel confident that if the noise in an aeroplane could be reduced to the level of that of a motorbus, for example, no other change or sign of progress would be required to ensure the doubling of the traffic within a year.[26]

Curiously enough, the figures issued by Imperial Airways shortly after this article was published showed that the number of passengers carried on the London–Paris route had almost doubled during 1932, rising from 4,167 (October 1930 to March 1931) to 7,733 (October 1931 to March 1932).

Quiet, of course, is a relative term. The express train and motorbus of the early 1930s were very noisy vehicles indeed, quite intolerable by modern standards, and, if travellers by air were to be provided with nothing better than this, the previous level of noise can certainly be reckoned to have been very bad indeed. But even so, the Heracles was regarded as a wonderfully luxurious aeroplane, with its two lavatories, inlaid wood panelling, comfortable armchairs and big windows. Even more impressive were the passenger-operated controls for heating and ventilation. 'In "Heracles" the occupant of each seat controls an inlet of cool air and a heating device in the floor that sends warm air up the legs of the sitter, most gratifying, I assure you.'[27]

There were, even so, certain pleasures which passengers had to deny themselves. One of them was smoking. This announcement appeared in the *Imperial Airways Gazette* in April 1936:

Rupert Belleville, of White's Club, St James's Street, W. was fined £10 and 3 guineas costs at Croydon Police Court on 17 March for smoking in the Imperial Airways liner *Heracles,* contrary to the regulations.

Belleville pleaded guilty. He was represented by Mr. St. John Hutchinson, K.C. Mr. Vincent Evans appeared for the Director of Public Prosecutions.

It was the first case of its kind in the world.

During the later 1930s, tremendous efforts were made to fill the rapidly increasing number of available seats. The pre-war airlines were worked very hard and their average loading around the year was certainly as good as it is today, on some routes much better. The salesmen neglected few opportunities. Honeymooners were urged to travel by air, with special emphasis on the saving of energy:

The great new airliners of Imperial Airways are the finest and most comfortable in the world, and travelling in them reduces fatigue to vanishing point – that's one of the reasons why ladies like air travel.

Simply telephone, and let us suggest some delightful alternative routes for a honeymoon by air. Why not put a return ticket by Imperial Airways amongst the items on your wedding list – to help your friends to send you a really useful wedding present?

> Just telephone
> VICTORIA 2211
> any time of the day or night[28]

27 Arrival at the Airport.
Croydon, 1928

28 The Moment of Truth.
Passenger-weighing
at Tempelhof, Berlin.
Mid-'thirties

Ladies were assured that they would find air travel particularly convenient, especially if they were travelling with children.

Travelling alone by air is easier for a woman than travelling alone by ship or train. Imperial Airways arranges everything for their special comfort.
There is a lavatory in every Imperial Airways Air Liner

Ladies should think in terms of air travel
Air travel offers you tremendous advantages, such as you never used to dream of. For instance, you can go to Paris and back in a day with time for social calls or business engagements in Paris. Arriving home, unfatigued, free from dust and dirt and as fresh as when you started, for it is much easier to look charming after an air journey than by any other form of travel.
Every newcomer to air travel is surprised at the SIMPLICITY. There is literally nothing to do but rest and enjoy the journey. The absence of fuss and formality always meets with favourable comment.

Complexions
Your complexion will not suffer during air travel, for one of the greatest features of flight is that everything is so clean – no dust, no dirt, you look, and are, as cool and fresh on arrival as when you started.

Children
Air travel offers you by far the healthiest and most comfortable travel for children and infants.
1. There is no fuss and hurly-burly about embarkation and disembarkation at Imperial Airways Air Ports.
2. The journey is so swift that children do not become tired and fretful and the aeroplane is never too cold or too warm. The child travels free from dust and dirt, and there is such a lot to interest them that they never have time to cry.[29]

Invalids in search of a cure were specially catered for:

Fly to PISTANY SPA,[30] famous for the successful treatment of RHEUMATISM, Arthritis, Neuritis, Sciatica, Lumbago, Gout, by Imperial Airways, Quickly and Comfortably. All services operated by 4-engined aircraft. Special facilities for invalids. 70% reduction on Return Fare for a stay of 3 weeks or more.
The Ala Certificate (price 7/6) entitles the holder to 70% reduction on the cost of the homeward journey.

Leave Croydon 09.45   Arrive Pistany 18.35
       Outward Journey   £12 10s. od.
       Homeward Journey   £3   15s. od.
(to holders of an Ala Certificate) Available until 2nd October

3 weeks stay, including cure costs at the two famous cure Hotels:

Grand Hotel Royal   £22
Thermia Palace Hotel   £31

Full information and Special Kronen Travellers' Cheques.[31]

Packaged holiday tours by air were coming in just before the outbreak of war in 1939. Among the companies advertising them were 'Cooks, Pickfords, Selfridge, LEP, LTA, Wakefield Fortune, Gondrands, Finnish, Wayfarers, Overseas League Travel, Mackay, American Express, Frames, Swans, Dean and Davisons, Bennets, Hickie Borman and Grants, Bedbrook and Page.'

Special trips were available to the Grand National:

The most famous airliner in the world – the Heracles takes you there and back in perfect comfort.

You leave town after breakfast and are back in time for dinner.

Special coach takes you from the airport to the course. The coach draws up in No. 1 enclosure – your grandstand for the race.

Light refreshments are served going and coming back during the flight.

5/– lunch baskets can be ordered in advance.

Ticket 8 guineas and inclusive of all transport, entrance to the course and light refreshments.

8.45	London Airway terminus
9.30	London Air Port
11.45 arr.	Speke (Liverpool) Air Port
1.15	Aintree race course
4.00	dep. Aintree race course
5.00	dep. Speke Air Port
7.00	arr. London Air Port
7.45	arr. London Airway terminus[32]

The many advertisements carried by newspapers in 1939 appeared under such headings as:

The Man who knows the value of time . . . flies
You can Fly to Hamburg in three hours
49 winks or 40 hours
15% reduction on air fares
Business houses save pounds on travel
To Hamburg and Back in a Day
Half Across Europe in Half a Day
Really modern transport
Europe at your feet
Five times faster transport
Speed without Hurry
Armchair to Europe

In the 'thirties, as in the 'twenties, the finest aviation prose continued, however, to be provided by the French airlines, as in this classic advice leaflet to passengers, issued by Lignes Aériennes Farman in 1930. Connoisseurs of airline publicity

29 To Central Europe in the mid-'twenties

should give themselves the pleasure of reading the French original[33] but the author's enthusiasm is not wholly obscured by translation.

When you are in an aeroplane, you have a completely different impression of the country over which you are flying. As you sit in your comfortable armchair, you can enjoy the wonderful panorama that spreads itself out below you. There is no rising ground, no trees or houses to hide the landscape from you. You can feast your eyes on everything at the same time, with points several kilometres distant clearly visible.

You would be quite wrong to think that the speed of the aeroplane interferes to the slightest degree with your pleasure. The landscape unrolls very slowly and you almost come to believe that your aircraft is hanging from the sky by an invisible thread. Actually, however, you are being carried along remarkably quickly, as you can discover for yourself merely by putting your hand out of the window.

Our routes link Paris with the main cities of Europe: Brussels, capital of bustling Belgium; Amsterdam, Venice of the North; Berlin, the great centre of the German-speaking world.

Don't imagine that travelling by air is ruinously expensive. The continuously increasing volume of our traffic has made it possible for us to reduce our prices to a point where we can challenge competition from the railways and offer you many special advantages at the same time.

Some passengers do, it is true, suffer from air-sickness, but there's no need to worry about this, because it's a mild affliction and, unlike seasickness, it can be easily avoided by taking Mothersills remedy.

Our aircraft are heated, but do, even so, bring a warm coat with you. There's absolutely no need for furs, goggles or special gloves.

You can have complete confidence in our pilots. We chose them very carefully. They're experts, and have families. Don't confuse commercial aeroplanes with the sporting variety. They're as different from one another as racing cars are from family saloons. We take every possible precaution for your safety. We operate within a network of weather forecasts, which ensures that your journey will take place in the best possible conditions, and radio allows our pilots to be kept continuously informed about the weather ahead.

Do you remember how the first railways were abused and ridiculed? And, in the same way, weren't the automobile pioneers reckoned to be completely mad?

Since 1928, improvements in air travel have been on such a scale that every reasonable person should now regard the aeroplane as a means of transport which is RAPID, CHEAP and NORMAL.

As faster aeroplanes came into service, some of the delightful customs which passengers had learnt to appreciate in earlier and more leisurely times disappeared. With flying time between London and Paris reduced to an hour and ten minutes by 1939, the five-course meals of the old Heracles days had to give way to snacks.

In the old, slow-flying days, when it was possible to see the ground below more easily, Imperial Airways issued their Silver Wing passengers with a ring-bound set of coloured flying maps of the London–Paris route.

The passenger maps should be read by looking along the 'black line route' in the direction of travel, i.e. hold the map with the line running away from you. Then you have a miniature of the country which you are passing over. At an average speed of 90 miles an hour, one side of a section will take approximately 14 minutes to cover.

In 1933 Imperial Airways introduced a new method of publicising the comfort of their services, the Tea Flight over London.

You would welcome a new and delightful experience? Then book your seat at once for an Afternoon Tea Flight over London in one of Imperial Airways' multi-engined luxury air liners! The same type as used on the Continental and Empire Services.
  A dainty tea will be served to you in your comfortable armchair in the air liner while London unrolls like a map before you. Every familiar landmark is there – yet looking quite different and new from your eagle's viewpoint.
  There is the familiar traffic – but crawling antwise and oddly. Here is the Tower. There is your own street! Look, Buckingham Palace! The Thames snakelike from Chelsea to its mouth. Wonderful! Fascinating beyond all describing.
  Try it for the sheer pleasure of the trip and also because there is no finer way of accustoming yourself to air travel, which is so much the quickest and most comfortable means of going to the Continent and the Empire that you will use it on every possible occasion when once you have experienced the joys of flight.[34]

The flights were operated every Friday and Sunday afternoon, 17 April to 30 September, then every Sunday to 18 December. Each flight lasted thirty minutes. Cars took passengers from the Airway terminus to Croydon and an inspection of the 'Air Port' and hangars preceded the flight. The cost was £1 10s. a head.

Some of the airlines went to considerable pains to discover what passengers thought of their services. An interesting report, based on customer-research, was published by Swissair in 1933. It concerned its Zurich–Vienna express service, for which a supplementary charge was made.

1. All passengers praised the punctuality of the service which aroused confidence and was adhered to with few exceptions.
2. No physical discomfort of any kind was felt by passengers as a result of the high flying speeds.
3. No cases of air sickness were reported, in spite of squally weather, as the machines do not roll and the length of flights was comparatively short, owing to the high speed.
4. Corpulent passengers wanted a somewhat larger cabin, like those they had been accustomed to in the case of the large triple-engined aeroplanes. The heaviest passenger, a gentleman from Zurich, was 120 kilos (18½ stone) in weight, but he had sufficient room next to 3 fellow passengers.[35]

Not all airlines were as fortunate in their customers. The London–Dublin service, which, somewhat surprisingly, was not eventually established until 1935, came in for some particularly harsh criticism. One passenger complained that there were no instructions about inflating and putting on the life-belt:

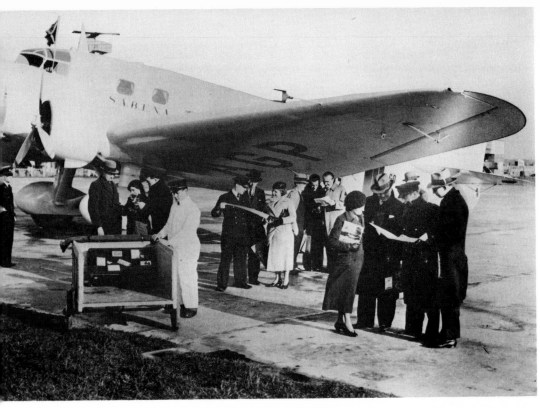

30 Brussels to Africa by Sabena Savoia Marchetti S.73, c. 1938. Studying the route-maps

It may be that the reason for this omission is that the Air Company felt that ample time will be given to the pilot to instruct all passengers before a descent is made, and that prior warning might make a nervous passenger more so. I do not agree with this. Does lifebelt and boat drill frighten passengers on board ship? No, surely on the contrary it gives them confidence.[36]

The plane windows were dirty, not even a cup of tea was to be had at the airport and the passengers became bored. The airline was lacking in enterprise in these matters.

In order to keep up the interest of the passenger, the cabin should be equipped with a speed indicator, clock and altitude meter. I vividly remember, as one of the party to Berlin in 1932, the keen interest which all took in these instruments fitted in the big Fokker in which we made the journey. Again, I feel that unless flying blind, it would add to the interest of things, were a roller blind, with place names thereon, adopted so that as one flew along, the more important places might be rolled into position. This could be accomplished by the assistant pilot without involving any great labour.[37]

This was not a typical reaction to flying, among the many thousands of people who were travelling each year. By 1939 the passengers had come to expect comfort, safety and reliability as normal. Nowhere was this more true than in the United States.

On the whole, Americans travelling by air in the 1930s seem to have been rather more interested in speed and reliability and rather less in luxurious comfort than the Europeans were. They were certainly not indifferent to comfort, however, and the airlines were always looking for new sales points. Pan American, for instance, provided special free socks with cardboard soles, to prevent passengers' feet from

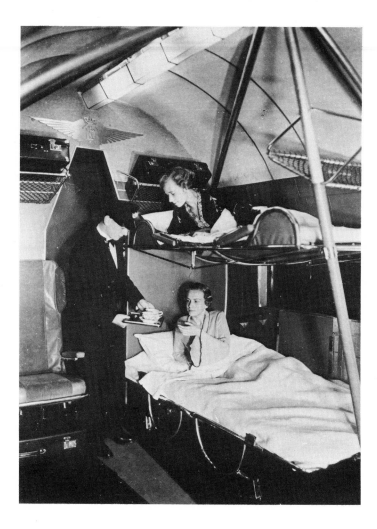

31 Night travel to the Far East. A KLM flight, c. 1937

swelling during flights. Few aircraft provided better conditions for passengers than the Douglas Sleeper Transport, brought into service in 1936, to carry sixteen people on long night journeys. The specification makes sad reading for anyone used to night flying nowadays:

The cabin will be 7 ft. 8 ins. wide and 6 ft. 6 ins. high, with eight roomy sections, four on each side of a broad aisle. Each section will have two seats, each 35 inches wide, facing each other. By night, the backs and bases of these seats will fold together to form a thick, soft foundation for the mattress of the lower berth. The upper berth and mattress will be dropped into position from the ceiling of the section. Each berth will measure 6 ft. 5 ins. in length – several inches longer than the standard railway sleeper berth – which will enable even a tall man to lie in complete comfort. The lower berth will measure 35 ins. wide and the upper berth 29 ins. The bottom of the lower berth will be 5 ins. above the floor, leaving a space for the storage of small hand luggage. The thick soft mattress and springs will add another 9 ins. to the height, holding the sleeping passenger 14 ins. above the floor of the cabin; the upper berth will be 46½ ins. above the floor, giving an ample clearance above the lower berth and steps will be provided to enable a passenger to enter this berth. The cabin windows will light the lower berth and a similar window, at the head, will provide light in the upper. Each berth will be complete with a reading light, a net for clothes, a baggage rack and a bell for calling the stewardess; separate dressing rooms will be provided for male and female passengers at the rear of the cabin and will be complete with running water, mirrors and towels. Toilet facilities will be provided at the rear of each dressing room. A very fully equipped pantry will be situated at the front of the cabin directly behind the pilot's cockpit and it will be possible to keep food hot or cold indefinitely without the use of thermos equipment.[38]

The most powerful tribute to the progress made by American aviation during the 1930s was not the Douglas Sleeper Transport, nor the number of passenger-miles flown each year, but the official acknowledgement made by the film industry in 1935 that flying could now be considered safe. Until then all American film stars were barred from flying by a special clause in their contracts. Their lives were considered by the film chiefs to be too precious for them to be allowed to take the the risk of going up in an aeroplane. The deletion of this clause was, perhaps, the most commercially valuable accolade the American aircraft industry has ever had.

3

The airships

THE FIRST practical airship was *La France*, built by Charles Renard and A. C. Krebs in 1884. She made seven flights, one of five miles. The early years of the twentieth century saw much development of dirigibles. In 1900 Count von Zeppelin flew his first big airship over Lake Constance. In 1901 Santos-Dumont took his *No. 6* round the Eiffel Tower and in 1903 the Lebaudy brothers piloted an airship thirty-eight miles, from Moisson to Paris.

Between 1910 and the outbreak of war in 1914 the five Zeppelins began passenger flights between German cities, carrying 35,000 people without any injury. These services were operated by the Deutsche Luftschiffahrts A. G. (Delag), which published a map in 1913 showing a circular route from the main base at Friedrichshafen, via Baden-Baden, Frankfurt-am-Main, Düsseldorf, Hamburg, Potsdam, Leipzig, Gotha and back to Friedrichshafen.

The airships built before and during the 1914–18 war were capable of remarkable performances. The Zeppelins operating in 1914 cruised at 32 knots, with a maximum speed of 45 knots, and could remain in the air for about 40 hours. Four years later the German *L72* was cruising at 49 knots, with a maximum speed of 66, and the endurance time had been raised to 182 hours at normal cruising speed.

In 1917 the Zeppelin *L57* covered 3,000 miles from Bulgaria to Khartoum and back with a full load of 10 tons of machine-guns, ammunition and medical stores, which were originally intended, before the airship was recalled, for supplying a garrison in East Africa. The flying time for the 3,000 miles was 97 hours.

In 1919 the British airship *R.34* put up an equally good performance across the Atlantic. She flew from Edinburgh to New York in 108 hours and back to Norfolk in only 75 hours.

Delag's first airship, the *LZ 7* (*Deutschland*), carried twenty-four passengers in a cabin which formed part of the main frame of the airship. The cabin was lined with plywood and carpeted. It had wicker seats and large windows, which could be opened. Like the later Zeppelins it had lavatories and washing facilities. The *Deutschland* crashed early in its career, but with no harm to the twenty-three journalists who were on board as passengers. Services were continued by the slightly older *LZ 6*, Delag's remaining airships, the *LZ 5* and *LZ 3*, having been taken over by the Ministry of War.

Delag did not operate after the war, but during the mid-1920s a new company, the Luftschiffbau Zeppelin, built the *LZ 127*, the *Graf Zeppelin*, which made its first flight in 1928. It flew to the United States in October of that year and subsequently cruised extensively over Europe and the Middle East, before making a round-the-world flight at the end of 1929, with a crew of forty-one and twenty passengers. Between 1930 and 1937 there were regular flights over the South Atlantic. It was then withdrawn from service, after carrying 13,100 passengers and making 144 ocean crossings.

The other great German airship of the years between the wars, *LZ 129* (*Hindenburg*), made its maiden flight in 1936. It was designed specifically for trans-oceanic services and carried fifty passengers, at a fare, for the single journey from Frankfurt to New Jersey or vice versa, of 450 dollars if a cabin was shared or 750 for a double cabin taken as a single. Its fastest flight took just under forty-three hours.

Hindenburg made ten round trips across the Atlantic during 1936, but in the following year, on 6 May, after the first of the 1937 crossings, the airship burst into flames and was completely destroyed while landing at Lakehurst, New Jersey. Thirty-six people lost their lives, the first passenger fatalities in the history of commercial airship operation. The cause of the disaster was never satisfactorily established, but the most likely explanation is that atmospheric electricity ignited hydrogen escaping from a leak in the airship.

The *Graf Zeppelin* could carry 150 passengers on day flights, but the normal total for trans-oceanic journeys was 50. The upper deck had 25 two-berth cabins, each with a wash-basin and clothes cupboard, down the centre, with a restaurant on the port side and a lounge and reading and writing room on the starboard side. A promenade area ran the full length of each outer side, with large windows angled outwards to provide a good view downwards. The windows could always be kept open because, due to the airflow round the hull, there were no draughts either inside or out. The lower deck contained a smoking room, bar, lavatories, shower bath, officers' mess, kitchen and crew mess. The decks were linked by two staircases.

The décor and furnishings of the *Graf Zeppelin* and the *Hindenburg* were lavish and fully up to the standard of the most modern transatlantic steamships. The lounge of the *Graf Zeppelin* had couches, curtained windows, flowers and a Japanese-style wallpaper. Tables in the lounge had lace-edged cloths on them and all the floors were carpeted. The public areas in the *Hindenburg* were even grander and will be described later.

The lavish meals would not have disgraced a major hotel on land. Menu cards[1]

32 The *Graf Zeppelin*. LZ 127 lands

from the *Graf Zeppelin* indicate what was provided. One of 1929 is headed on the first page 'First World's Tour; the Graf Zeppelin' and has a picture captioned 'Soaring over Los Angeles Biltmore'. Inside is:

On Board Airship
Graf Zeppelin
Los Angeles to Lakehurst

First Luncheon
Honey Dew Melon au Citron
Hungarian Goulash
Cold Asparagus Vinaigrette
Eclairs
Coffee

and the name of the creators of the meal, 'Los Angeles Biltmore, Caterers'.

For flights out of Germany, local restaurateurs were employed. A menu card of 1933, for a flight to the Chicago World's Fair, is headed: *An Bord des Luftschiffes Graf Zeppelin*. On top of the card is a picture of the earth, the Zeppelin and three flags. Then come the words 'Fahrt zur Welt. Austellung Chicago 1933. Bewirtschaftung. Kurgarten Hotel Friedrichshafen.' After that is the menu, which would certainly have had to be followed by a walk on the promenade deck:

Schildkroetensuppe

–oOo–

Fischschnitten nach
Helgoland   Salzkartoffel

–oOo–

Ochsenlende englisch gebraten
fein garniert
gruener Salat

–oOo–

Bueckler Eiscreme
Kleingebaeck

A very full description of the amenities and arrangements on the *Hindenburg* has been provided by an American passenger.[2]

Passengers boarded the airship via the lower deck, B deck. When they reached the top of the noble staircase to A deck, they were confronted by a bust of Field Marshal Paul von Hindenburg. Ahead of them at this point were the twenty-five cabins. These being in the centre of the ship, there were no windows, 'a cause of some complaint, particularly to those who had flown in the "Graf Zeppelin" and could remember how they could lie in their berths with a full view of the horizon through the windows'. However, the nine cabins added during the winter of 1936–37 did have windows and were much sought after. Each cabin had two berths, one above the other.

Above each berth was an ingenious no-smoking sign – a lighted cigarette with a slender sprite of smoke spiraling therefrom – and then, the whole seductive picture *crossed out* with a half inch red paint brush. On the door jamb were three push buttons – the lower one identified by a wine glass. When you pushed it, a drink was produced. This saved walking perhaps 50 feet to the handiest of the three bars that were maintained by the 7 stewards all day and most of the night. . . . We disremember what the other two buttons were for. The berths were comfortable, but anyone not used to sleeping under the German-style puff that they used instead of blankets will find parts of his anatomy exposed to the cooling blast of the ventilator some time during the night. The eiderdown quilts matched the color scheme of the walls, which were light blue, grey or beige. The traveler might not at first notice that for the sake of lightness the walls of the state-rooms were of a lightweight composition covered with airship fabric – soundproofed sufficiently to prevent understanding what is said in the next room, but one of the crew playing the accordion on the deck below added a pleasant note. The cabin door slid in guides – its weight, or rather its lack of weight – is the first impression one receives as to how lightly any part not contributing to the structure of the airship is built.

Passengers had to observe regulations strictly:

Breakfast was served from 8 to 10 am, luncheon after 12 noon, afternoon tea at 4 pm, and dinner at 7. The public rooms were generally to be closed at 11 pm, though some might continue to make merry in the bar and smoking room on B deck – here is where the cheery souls stay – until 3 am. The lighting of matches as well as smoking is strictly forbidden on board the airship as well as in its vicinity. Only in the designated smoking room of the airship *Hindenburg* is smoking permitted. Because of restrictions by the governments of the countries over which the Zeppelin flew, passengers were obliged to surrender their cameras to the ship's personnel for safe-keeping. Outside the 3-mile limit they might get them back, and photograph the ocean. Every traveler is therefore required, in his own and in the general interest, to obey the orders of the captain, or of his representative. The chief steward would arrange for passengers to charge drinks, which were not to be paid for at the bar, and would cash checks in limited amounts in payment for drinks, postcards and souvenirs. Tips for the stewards were included in the fare. Arrangements could be made through the chief steward to send telegrams via the ship's radio station. A small library in the lounge would issue books against receipts, and passengers were cautioned not to leave them in public rooms. A sick bay attendant was on board who would care for and provide medication without cost to passengers (for the 1937 season the owners, the Deutsche Zeppelin Reederei, shipped a physician, Dr Rüdiger, who survived the Lakehurst disaster). The passengers were requested to prevent damage to the machinery installations abaft the passenger spaces, not to throw objects out of the windows.

The public rooms were remarkable:

As an advertisement for the opulence and taste of the New Germany, the talents of the

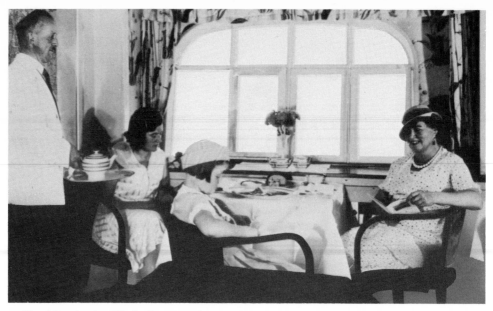

33 Breakfast in the *Hindenburg*, 1936

country's most famous architects and artists had been exploited. The largest rooms were on A deck outboard of the passenger cabins. To port, occupying an area measuring 15 × 50 feet, was the dining room. Here, with all the luxury and refinement of a small restaurant, were seats for 34 passengers – at four small tables for two persons along the inboard wall, and at six larger tables outboard. The tables – and the chairs likewise – were of a special lightweight tubular aluminium design – as light as possible, as stable as possible – created for the *Hindenburg* by Professor Breuhaus. In the dining room the chairs were upholstered in red. The inner walls, covered with airship cotton fabric and off-white in color, bore 21 original paintings by Professor Arpke. This gentleman did not interpret his contract to decorate the public rooms to mean that he was to create a flying picture gallery, but rather he was conscious of the fact that his pictures were not an end in themselves, but should enliven the rooms. His work therefore was to correspond with the nature of the airship and to be related to air travel. Thus, the colorful paintings in the dining room represent *Graf Zeppelin* on a South American journey, departing Friedrichshafen, passed over the Spannish coast, the African landscape, the Cape Verde and Canary Islands, a full rigged ship on the wide wastes of the ocean, soaring gulls, sharks in the azure water, the island of Fernando Noronha, desolate St. Paul's Rocks in the middle of the South Atlantic, the palms and surf of the coast of South America, butterflies, fishing natives and finally, Rio and the Sugar Loaf on the rim of its incomparable harbor.

The table arrangements were impeccable:

The tables were laid with white linen napkins and tablecloths, fresh-cut flowers, fine silver and the special china service created for the *Hindenburg*. I am fortunate enough

68

to own a demitasse cup and saucer from this set – a gift of the widow of the late General-major Joachim Breithaupt, former Airship Adviser in the German Air Ministry. Ex-quisitely confected of 'Heinrich Ivory Porcelain', it is marked on the bottom, 'Property of the German Zeppelin *Reederei*', bears a chased gold and blue band around the rim, and exhibits the *Reederei* crest and a white Zeppelin outlined in gold, superimposed on a blue globe with meridians of longitude and parallels of latitude in gold.

[On the starboard side] the wall of the lounge bore a huge Mercator projection of the world, depicting the ships and sea voyages of Columbus, Vasco da Gama, Magellan and Cook, the North Atlantic route of the German express liners *Bremen* and *Europa*, the Atlantic crossing of the LZ126 *Los Angeles*, the world flight of the *Graf Zeppelin* and her passenger route to South America. Tables and chairs – these upholstered in brown – furnished the room, and in a corner was the surprise of surprises, a Blüthner baby grand piano, its weight kept down to 397 pounds through the use of aluminium, and finished in yellow pigskin. This, after some soul-searching, was provided as a concession to veteran airship passengers who complained that a piano was all that was lacking in the convivial parties aboard the old *Graf Zeppelin*. The gray-walled writing and reading room was decorated with eleven more of Professor Arpke's paintings showing the developement [sic] of postal services, from the Chinese foot messenger and Eskimo dog sled to the express steamer, the mail plane, and finally the *Graf Zeppelin*. Pneumatic tubes enabled letter writters to send their missives direct to the mail room above the control car.

The promenade decks were one of the greatest attractions of a Zeppelin voyage:

Outboard of the public rooms, and separated from them by a low railing, were 50-foot promenades connected by a cross-passage between the two sides of A deck. This afforded a walking distance of nearly 200 feet for transatlantic passengers used to the daily consti-tutional around a steamer deck. Outboard of the promenades were six large Plexi-glass windows, slanting outwards at 45°, often left open as there was no draft in or outwards even at an air speed of 80 knots. Here the passengers stood or sat for hours on low cushioned seats, enthralled by the sight of foaming waves, tossing ships, forests, towns, rivers and cities, going by only a few hundred feet below. Curtains drawn at night between the promenade and public rooms enabled the travelers to enjoy the sight of moonlight on the waves, the brilliance of the stars, without the glare and reflection of the artificial lighting.

On *Hindenburg*, in great contrast to the aeroplanes of the day, smoking was permitted, although with strict safeguards:

Sheer fantasy was the word for the smoking room forward on the starboard side of B deck. For a hydrogen-filled airship this was a startling feature, yet safety was assured through the $12\frac{1}{2} \times 15\frac{1}{2}$ foot room being pressurised against the entrance of hydrogen, and sealed off by an air-lock door. This was under the control of the bar steward, whose duty it was to inspect each guest to make sure that he was not carelessly departing with a burning cigarette, cigar or pipe. The steward also was the sole custodian of matches. 'In the smoking room,' noted one reporter, 'is *one* electric lighter of the automobile type. This proves rather tough for cigar smokers (and Germans are partial to fairly good cigars) and impossible for pipe addicts. In the latter case, the smoke room steward, with a rather reluctant mien, may be approached on his off side, and persuaded to produce and ignite one (1) lucifer (or match) to the offending pipe-bowl; but he retains hold of said match with great tenacity, from ignition to charred cinder. For the passenger to do his own lighting is *streng verboten*.'

And yet, despite all these attentions to his welfare, the transatlantic passenger still found it possible to be bored and other means of keeping him amused had to be found:

One diversion was the tour of the ship. Passengers could expect to be conducted at least once through the keel in groups of three, guided by the chief steward. None failed to be impressed by the vast dimensions of the gas cells, the quantities of stores, fuel and water carried on each side of the narrow catwalk, and the reassuring presence of the spare engine and reserve propellers – all lending a sense of permanence and purpose.

The *Hindenburg* and the *Graf Zeppelin* had no competitors. What they achieved was never achieved again, although for some years the British tried to keep in the race. Vickers built airships from 1908 to 1929, the last being the *R.100*. In the *R.100* the passenger and crew accommodation was arranged within the lower hull in three decks nearer to the bow. The dining saloon seated fifty-six. It was on the centre deck and had a viewing promenade 40-feet long on either side. A staircase led up from the dining saloon to a gallery lounge. The cabins, for a total of 100 passengers, were on the middle and upper decks. They had either two or four berths.[3] 'The walls dividing the cabins were of fabric, so that a man snoring in the next cabin could be a real nuisance at night; so quiet was the ship.'[4]

The situation in the airship world at that time was curious [wrote Nevil Shute]. It was generally agreed in 1924 that the aeroplane would never be a very suitable vehicle for carrying passengers across the oceans, and that airships would operate all the long-distance routes of the future. We were all quite wrong, of course, but at that time it seemed reasonable; no aeroplane had yet succeeded in crossing the Atlantic from east to west, whereas a German airship, the Graf Zeppelin, was already carrying commercial loads of passengers both ways to South America upon a regular schedule. In England Sir Dennis Burney was perhaps the leading airship enthusiast, acting with Vickers Ltd., and in 1923 this group put forward a proposal to the Government that they should build six commercial airships and set up a company to operate them on the Empire routes. This proposal was approved in principle, but before an agreement could be signed and sealed the Conservative Government went out and the first Labour Government came in, and the whole thing was thrown back into the melting pot.[5]

The decision arrived at was a curious one. The Government said, in effect, 'The Air Ministry at Cardington shall build an airship of a certain size, load-carrying capacity, and speed, and Vickers Ltd. shall build another one to the same contract specification. By this ingenious device we shall find out which is the better principle, capitalism or State enterprise.'[6]

Previous airships built in Britain had been built without proper theoretical knowledge. The usual method was to study the wreckage of the German airships shot down over France or England and to copy the size of the girders, without making any attempt to calculate the aerodynamic stresses. The *R.38* broke in two for this reason.

During the experimental flight which *R.100* made to Canada in 1930, one of the technical staff noted that 'Sleep all night in bed, get up, shave in hot water, dress and eat a breakfast served in a Christian way. If this water collector can be developed, as I think it can, we may be able to have baths in future ships.'[7]

On the other hand, airships were normally unheated, since heating presented technical problems which were difficult to overcome. Stability was not always what it might have been hoped. Over Montreal the nose dipped at least 35 degrees and supper shot off the table, finishing up thirty feet down the corridor.[8]

R.100 never flew again. She was broken up for scrap, after the disaster to the *R.101*, her sister ship. The *R.101* broke her back, caught fire and crashed in a thunderstorm near Beauvais, at the beginning of an ill-judged flight to India. All the people on board were killed in the accident. Fare-paying passengers never had an opportunity to enjoy the comfort of a British-built airship.

34 America's first flying workhorse. The Ford 2AT, c. 1930

4

Air travel in the 'twenties and 'thirties

THE GENERAL strategy of selling air travel was clearly laid down in the 1920s. The airlines would compete as soon as they were in a position to prove to potential passengers that the services they had to offer were based on speed, reliability, safety and comfort. Given this as a basis, the salesmen and public relations departments should be able to discover the customers without too much difficulty. To begin with the emphasis was, quite understandably, on safety, on assuring passengers that they would survive their flights. Thus, in the United States in the mid-1920s, with the development of domestic air services still lagging behind Europe, it was pointed out that, on British and Dutch airliners during 1921–23 the passenger air-miles per fatality were 2,663,000, while on the New York Central Railroad in 1923 the number of passenger train-miles per passenger casualty (killed or injured) was 4,400,000.[1] The implication was that the airlines still had some way to go before they were entitled to complete trust from the public.

The following year the *Washington Post* made the same point even more strongly in an editorial.

An official of a passenger air service company makes the significant statement that air transportation can never take its proper place beside the railroad and steamship until the public is convinced that it can be carried not only in perfect safety but also with reasonable assurance of comfort and punctuality Apparently the organisations engaged in pioneering transport through the air realise that their biggest task is the winning of public confidence.

Not many years ago both the railroad and the steamship were confronted by a similar problem. . . . Eventually, however, the public will accept air transportation in a matter of fact manner as any other method of travel. . . . Public confidence in air transportation seems to be not very far around the corner.[2]

This corner was turned within four or five years after the *Washington Post* produced its warning, but it is important to remember that the meaning of reliability, safety, speed and comfort varied a good deal, according to the area of the world in which one lived. In Central Africa or the Soviet Far East, for example, there was no point in making comparisons between aeroplanes and Pullman

D

trains, since there were no Pullman trains, whereas in the United States such a comparison was very natural.

Australia was in something of a middle position. Parts of the continent had rail services and parts had not. The early sales-literature put out by the national airline, Qantas, is therefore interesting to study. The cover of a booklet issued in 1928 emphasises time, 'Save days of travel by using Qantas mail and taxi-planes', and money, 'Cost compares favourably with railway travel'. 'Flights on any section of the route', it said, 'show a large saving over other means of transport, this being particularly valuable to travellers in Western Queensland, where the distances are great and the rail services are slow and disconnected. Road travel by car is good in dry weather, but is completely suspended following heavy falls of rain. Air travel is, therefore, the most speedy and also the most reliable means of transport.'

Figures were given to show the advantages of air over rail travel:

INSTANCES OF SAVINGS

	Rail	By Air Connection
Charleville–Longreach	4½ days	4 hrs.
Longreach–Cloncurry	3 days	4 hrs. 30 mins.
Cloncurry–Camooweal	3 days	3 hrs. 30 mins.
Longreach–Sydney	76 hrs.	52 hrs.
Camooweal–Sydney	9 days	4 days
Brisbane–Normanton	11 days	2 days 20 hrs.

Cost – Passenger fares on the regular route range from 7*d.* to 9*d.* per mile, according to the distance travelled. These charges in instances compare favourably with rail fares, owing to the direct air line flown from point to point and to the travelling expenses [i.e. the cost of hotels and meals *en route*] saved by taking the direct route.

COMPARISON OF COST

	Rail	By Air
Charleville–Longreach	£11 19 6	£8 10 0
Longreach–Cloncurry (plus travelling expenses)	8 12 0	10 0 0

The saving in travel time also has a cash value to the majority of passengers.

It was also suggested that air travel was more comfortable:

The fact that medical men in Longreach, Charleville and Cloncurry had advised their patients time and again to travel only by air, and that many invalids have used our facilities, including people with weak hearts, women just out of hospital, and infants three weeks old, demonstrates the ease of air travel.

When the shade temperature stands at 115° the traveller naturally turns from the dusty road and the wearisome heat of the railway coach to aerial travel, where the journey can be undertaken in temperatures of from 70° to 75°.

The adjustment of special cabin ventilators enables passengers to enjoy a warm and comfortable trip during winter months.

Passengers are invited to test the difference between reading or writing in a train or car and in a modern aeroplane.

A number of the Australian pioneers have recorded their memories of flying in the early days. One of them, Arthur H. Affleck, flew Qantas planes for a number of years in the 1920s and also had a good deal of experience of the Flying Doctor service:

Even in the early days[3] of airline operation with the only alternative means of transport days of bumping over dusty, potholed roads, followed by an equally uncomfortable train journey, the travelling public was beginning to look for at least a certain degree of comfort and convenience. However, the passenger paid for his own accommodation and meals en route and it was only by purest chance that he was ever provided with a cup of tea at any of the intermediate stopping places. It was to take many years before the fare-paying airline passenger was provided with inclusive meals and a hostess service.

At no one of the hotels where we stayed overnight did the publican consider it worth-while to supply early breakfast to passengers or crew, and the pilot, in addition to flying the aircraft and, in many instances, refuelling and servicing it, was required to wake his passengers, rush down to the hotel kitchen and make a cup of tea and toast for them, help handle their baggage, collect mails from the local post-office and freight from the agent's office, pick up any other passengers from their homes or other hotels, and then get out to the aerodrome in time to open up the hangar, push the aircraft out with the assistance of any of the passengers who felt strong enough to help at that hour of the day, start up, load up and take off at the first crack of dawn.[4]

On the service from Cloncurry to Normanton, passengers

. . . were required to make themselves as comfortable as possible jammed into a cabin with, amongst other items, three or four large cornsacks full of wriggling and twitching fish. Our normal weekly fishy load weighed in the vicinity of 500–600 lbs. and when, in addition to this, there were two or three passengers, suitcases, swags, saddles, rifles, mailbags, sundry items of freight and a couple of savage cattle dogs travelling with their drover master, all to be fitted into a small four-seater cabin, the resultant congestion needed to be seen to be believed.[5]

Another early Qantas pilot, Hudson Fysh,[6] recalls the delights of flying a

Bristol Fighter in 1923:

The engine was lubricated by pure castor oil, the smell of which enveloped the pilot with its subtle fumes and made him and his clothes smell, as was the case with all true pilots trained on rotary engines. As for the passengers, they hated it – but who amongst the pilots worried about the passengers in those days? Almost every one of them got sick.[7]

In the public mind, one Qantas pilot was certainly not interchangeable with another:

Back in the 1920s a great many people would fly only with pilots they knew and trusted – pilots who were never seen beating it up at their night stops and that sort of thing. Also, when insuring aircraft against accident, the ruling rate being 10 to 12 per cent per annum on the value of the aeroplane, the insurance company always wanted to know who the pilots were. Each pilot had his risk rating.

A story is told about the time Moody went on leave and a new pilot from the old country, Russell Tapp, took over in his place. He had rather an English voice and a fresh complexion. We had DH. 61s then, and George Herriman, our Charleville agent, came out to the aerodrome with a passenger booked for Longreach. On went his luggage, and the passenger looking round said 'Where's Skipper Moody?' 'Oh,' said Herriman, 'he's on leave. Come and I'll introduce you to the new pilot.' The introduction being over, the passenger got the jitters on being asked to board the plane, and exclaimed, 'Not on your life! Not for me – I'm not going. Take my luggage out.' And go he did not, returning to Charleville to make the four-day journey round to Longreach by train instead of the few hours by air.[8]

There was no insurance of any kind for the passengers, Hudson Fysh remembers:

We had no aircraft accident insurance, the rates being prohibitive, no third party cover, and in regard to passenger liability we relied on the ticket signed by each passenger, which stated that they travelled at their own risk. In the case of minors, the next of kin signed.[9]

In the 'twenties Qantas operated only in outback western Queensland, where the people were still somewhat rugged pioneers and not used to feather-bedding. The passengers using Qantas services included pastoralists, sheep men, cattle men, drovers (who would bring back their saddles and their dog as their only luggage), doctors, sick people needing medical or hospital treatment, local lawyers, magistrates, sheep and cattle dealers, some commercial travellers and itinerant salesmen, and with the discovery of the big silver mines at Mt Isa an increasing number of mining and technical engineering people. From the outset womenfolk travelled (many with babies) to avoid the three-day primitive railway journey, and comprised perhaps 20 per cent. of travellers. Throughout the 1920s a sprinkling of children travelled unaccompanied to or from their boarding-schools, since their parents often lived on sheep or cattle properties remote from even country townships.

In 1924–26 the mail planes D.H.9C) had capacity for three passengers and the pilot. All of them wore cap and goggles, a selection of these articles being carried on the aircraft. From 1926 to 1927 the mail aircraft were mostly the four-passenger D.H.50A which had a semi-enclosed box cabin for passengers and obviated the need for wearing a cap and goggles. By 1929 most of the D.H.50As had been replaced by the larger single-engined D.H.61s, which carried nine passengers and provided, for the first time, a lavatory.

The pre-1939 pilots, emphasised Captain Lester Brain[10] (who flew for Qantas throughout the 'twenties and 'thirties) had to be well-equipped with the public relations skills and were proud to be more than mere pilots. 'I only wish', he said in his retirement, 'that all pilots of today felt that way, instead of giving the impression that somehow they are God's chosen few, successors to the saviours of Britain, and that the rest of the population owes them a luxurious, secure living and princely retirement allowance.'

In the earliest days passengers were actually grateful. The habit of criticism came later, with the more advanced aircraft. 'In the 1920s', Captain Brain remembers, 'passengers accepted the primitive facilities without grumbling. It was not really until, say, 1938, with the introduction of the then luxurious Empire Flying Boat Services that travellers grumbled and criticised the food, the overnight accommodation and so on.'

Under Australian conditions air travel might, in certain circumstances, be the only possibility. One such instance is remembered by Mr N. A. Parkes, who lives in Queensland. In 1925 his mother, who suffered from asthma, was living with him on a property he managed in Western Queensland, where the air was very dry. He wrote later:

For two years Mrs Parkes got great relief during the winter but could not stand the summer heat. The third year, 1927, she became seriously ill with abscesses in the gall duct. My sister Mrs G. Davison came to help nurse our mother.

In September after a spell of hot weather the doctor warned us that our mother would not survive another. To take her to Sydney by train meant the risk she would die on the journey.

We appealed to Qantas and Mr Fysh, then resident in Longreach, undertook to supply a plane to fly us to Sydney.

The plane to seat six had four seats removed and replaced with a stretcher, leaving a seat for my sister and myself.

The plane, flown by pilot Stewart, landed on a claypan close to Aldringham house in the evening and next morning we started off early. Landed at Longreach and Charleville to re-fuel and stayed overnight at Bourke. Our mother stayed in the plane overnight. Next morning the plane was hard to start and the writer pulled the propeller round for over an hour before it started. We landed at Dubbo, then Mascot, where an ambulance met us to take the patient to Eastwood. The only part of the trip that in any way distressed her was in the ambulance.[11]

The situation over much of the Soviet Union was very similar:

Aircraft used for ambulance work were brought under one control in August 1934 when the Health Department was supplied with a number of aircraft with facilities for the carriage of patients, doctors and nurses. Despite the difficulties under which the squadron worked, between the 1st August 1934 and the 1st November of the same year, aircraft flew 110,000 kilometres (68,354 miles), carried sixty-three patients, thirty-four doctors, and conveyed 1,000 kilograms of medical supplies. . . . There is no state in the whole world in which the rapid introduction of air transport was so desirable as in the Soviet Union. The large area governed by one administration and the inadequate road and rail communications provided ample reason for the success of air transport. The regularity of the air services has not yet attained anything like the regularity of European air services but the cause of this lies in the considerable climatic differences. A further reason for irregularity is the material used, but great improvements are being made. Average speeds are well behind those customary in Europe, on the main routes being (including landings) in the region of 87 kilometres (54 miles) an hour and rising to 140 kilometres (87 miles) an hour on the international routes. As emphasised before, speed must be valued comparatively. When an air service has to compete with an efficient railway system giving speeds of 90 kilometres an hour, it must attain an average of at least 200 kilometres an hour, for interruption of the services at night must be taken into account. If, on the other hand, an air service has as its sole competitor horse-drawn vehicles or water transport, working on an average speed of not more than 10 kilometres an hour as is the case on many routes in the U.S.S.R., a speed of 100 kilometres an hour offers relatively greater advantages than a speed of 200 kilometres an hour does, for example, in America. It must be remembered, too, that an air service working on an average speed of 100 kilometres an hour is more than proportionately cheaper than one working on a speed of 200 kilometres an hour. These special conditions existing in the U.S.S.R. have given rise to the study of very slow aircraft as well as fast and relatively uneconomic aircraft.[12]

Where the alternative means of transport was no transport at all, the marketing of air travel was a meaningless activity. Once an air service became available, it was used. The service sold itself. In other countries, however, where aeroplanes had to fight their way against competition from surface transport, passengers had to be persuaded that it was to their advantage to fly.

Saving of time was usually pushed as the greatest benefit. An interesting example of this appeal, during the 1920s, is to be found in the system developed by the Ukrainian Air Transport Company. This airline was founded in 1923 and its aim was to provide rapid passenger and parcel services between Moscow and the most important centres in the Ukraine, Charkow, Odessa and the Donbass.

The system was that at railway stations and river ports which were on the air routes, people who wanted to fly simply had to equip themselves with the respective railway tickets for the journey and then if they wanted to fly on the aeroplane instead, they could.

The possession of a ticket gave the passengers the right to take with them hand luggage to a maximum of 5 kilogrammes on inland routes and 10 kilogrammes on the route to Persia. Every passenger was insured automatically for 5,000 roubles. His ticket also served as an insurance policy. If a plane had to make a forced landing and it proved impossible to continue the flight, passengers were refunded the cost of a railway ticket to their destination.

Before the coming of aeroplanes, travel within the Soviet Union was notoriously slow, even by rail. This fact was well known to international travellers and one need look no further for the reason for the success of the joint Russian-German airline, Deruluft, which began a passenger service between Berlin and Moscow in 1925 and continued to operate until 1937. Deruluft had started flying operations in May 1922. To begin with there was a bi-weekly mail service flown by German pilots between Königsberg and Moscow. This was increased to three times weekly in 1923, but mail and what were tactfully termed 'diplomatic couriers' were carried. In 1924, when there were daily flights, ordinary passengers were taken and in the following year Berlin was linked to Moscow by the opening of a Deutscher Aero Lloyd service, Berlin–Danzig–Königsberg, to connect with the Deruluft service.

During the summer months Deruluft sometimes flew Königsberg–Berlin and Moscow–Khakov. Regular night flights between Berlin and Königsberg were introduced in 1927 and a northern route, Königsberg–Riga–Tallinin–Leningrad, was opened in 1928.

In 1922 it took $10\frac{1}{2}$ hours to fly from Moscow to Königsberg, the fare being quoted as 75 US dollars. In 1934 the Moscow–Berlin flight lasted 11 hours, which was about a third of the time taken by the train. The number of passengers understandably grew quickly and the planes were nearly always full. In 1932, 3,610 passengers were carried, in 1933 5,857 and in 1934 12,130.[13] This, too, was a service which presented no sales problem to the operators.

Most of the world's airlines, however, had been faced, from the beginning, with the need to work hard to fill more than 50 per cent. of their seats, taken on a round-the-year average, and with the knowledge that all the profit lay in the second 50 per cent. Some of them pursued a more consistently aggressive and intelligent sales policy than others. It is not over-patriotic to say that Imperial Airways displayed exceptional enterprise in their pre-1939 marketing policy. They knew the kind of people they were aiming at and they devoted a great deal of imagination and energy to get them as passengers.

One thinks, for instance, of the cigarette-card campaign, launched in 1936 in co-operation with Lambert and Butler, a branch of the Imperial Tobacco Company. This series of fifty coloured cards went into packets of 'Waverley' and 'Rhodian' cigarettes. They showed maps, airliners and pictures of important places along the routes to Africa and Australia. Another idea, used by both Imperial Airways and KLM, was to issue passengers with a signed, postcard-size picture of their pilot. Regular travellers built up a collection of these and the pilots became well-known figures as a result.

In the mid-1930s Imperial Airways developed what they called 'A Certificate of Contemporary Travel', with the aim of creating a club-feeling among passengers on the South Africa route. The certificate was bordered with African jungle scenes

35 Personalising the pilot: an Imperial Airways postcard of the mid-'thirties

LAMBERT & BUTLER'S CIGARETTES

"HANNO" AT BAGHDAD AIRPORT

LAMBERT & BUTLER'S CIGARETTES

LONDON
PARIS
BRINDISI
ATHENS
ALEXANDRIA
BAGHDAD
BAHREIN
KARACHI
DELHI
CALCUTTA
RANGOON
BANGKOK
PENANG

ENGLAND—INDIA—MALAYA—
AUSTRALIA ROUTE MAP A

LAMBERT & BUTLER'S CIGARETTES

ARCH OF CTESIPHON, IRAQ

LAMBERT & BUTLER'S CIGARETTES

REFUELLING "SCIPIO" IN ALEXANDRIA HARBOUR

LAMBERT & BUTLER'S
CIGARETTES

"HANNO" AT MUHARRAK, PERSIAN GULF

LAMBERT & BUTLER'S CIGARETTES

JERUSALEM—THE TEMPLE AREA

LAMBERT & BUTLER'S CIGARETTES

"HANNO" AT SHARJAH, PERSIAN GULF

LAMBERT & BUTLER'S CIGARETTES

"HANNO" OVER THE DEAD SEA

LAMBERT & BUTLER'S
CIGARETTES

"HANNO" AT GWADAR, BALUCHISTAN

LAMBERT & BUTLER'S CIGARETTES

EL KADIMAIN MOSQUE, BAGHDAD

and had an aeroplane flying overhead. It registered the fact that the passenger, whose name was written into the appropriate space by the pilot,

> has flown over the equator in the *Empire* flying boat the_____thus becoming one of the progressive band of travellers who cross the line by air. Over the waters of Lake Victoria, the Lingge Archipelago, the *Empire* flying boats pass in a moment from hemisphere to hemisphere, beyond the zone whose dwellers recognise no alteration in the length of night and day.

> 'Born with the sun they travelled a short way towards the sun,
> And left the vivid air signed with their honour'

Stephen Spender

Longitude _____
Latitude zero _____
_____ 193 _____
_____ Cdr.

From 1935 onwards KLM presented each passenger on the Amsterdam – Batavia service with a copy of E. Rusman's *Wings Across Continents*, a hard-cover book of 100 pages, well illustrated, which sets out in considerable detail what could be seen at the places chosen for overnight stops. The realistic and often far from romantic descriptions give a clue to the kind of passenger KLM expected to travel on their service. Here is an example of the approach:

Baghdad, once a city of fairy-tales has indeed fallen upon evil days, and the spirit of Haroun al Raschid no longer hovers over it. Here and there in the dirty, noisy streets one obtains a glimpse, in some narrow alley, of a flower-bright inner court with a tinkling fountain beneath a lemon tree, and it is true that there is a Biblical dignity about the goat herds outside the city near the aerodrome. For the rest, Baghdad is a nightmare of incongruity, where all of the west that is slovenly has been adopted by the east. Beside a heavily laden ass rattles an equally heavily laden Ford of ancient design and the women no longer draw water from age-old wells in slender earthen jars, but in petrol tins! The painted wooden houses are patched with rusty corrugated iron and only the gufa, that tubby, circular boat which the ancient Assyrians used upon the Tigris, has remained unchanged and in daily use for perhaps 60 centuries or more.

The book has good maps and at the back, to convince the traveller that he had made no mistake when he decided to fly KLM, are two pages of testimonials from satisfied customers. One of these, from the Editor of the *Kölnische Illustrierte Zeitung*, is somewhat ambiguously worded – 'It was an indescribable experience and I notice that only little by little I begin to realise what it was all like' – but the general tone is that of the comment by Lord Moyne and Lady Broughton, 'famous big game hunters'. They testified

> We have made a perfect journey to Rangoon in PH-AIQ with absolute punctuality and at high speed. Nothing could have exceeded the consideration of Captain Smirnoff and his crew and the perfection of their arrangements to make our flight interesting and comfortable. I would especially commend the seating arrangements of the aeroplane which have prevented any feeling of fatigue during the seven days we have spent on board.

The American airlines, too, made much use of the testimonial. One, publicised in the late 1930s, was from A. D. Hoseason, M.D., England. It read

> During a recent visit to the United States, my wife and I travelled a considerable distance by TWA. We wish to say that we were greatly impressed by the efficiency with which your flights are conducted, including the ground organisation and safety precautions. We also appreciated the point that on TWA passengers can reserve their seating accommodation.
>
> I have flown most European air lines, and also in Africa, and I consider that from the point of view of the passenger's comfort – (free meals, endless supplies of coffee, newspapers and especially a trained nurse as hostess) – American Civil Flying is years in advance of most airlines this side of the Atlantic.

On the whole, however, the American approach was to stress the good value for money and the technical innovations which their services offered. For the DC-1, for instance, it was announced by TWA that the seats 'were designed to their own specifications and are adjustable to any comfortable position. They are reversible, permitting passengers to face the rear if desired. This feature alone offered the answer to requests of many passengers that seats be arranged so that passengers can face each other and converse freely and could also permit card-playing while in flight.'

In 1939 the emphasis was on radio broadcasts during flights. This apparatus was installed on twenty-two DC-3s. Passengers got their radio via a receiver controlled by the stewardess. An undated TWA memorandum of this year reads:

> Individual loudspeakers will be provided [sic] passengers upon request. The individual speakers will be plugged into outlets on each seat and then fastened to the back-rest to provide individual reception for each passenger.
>
> The radios will also be connected to cockpits of planes to inaugurate the first standard practice of pilot announcements to passengers regarding flight location, altitude, arrival time at airports, and other comments of general interest.
>
> Hostesses controlling the master receiving unit will tune in on stations near the plane's course and offer programs appealing to the majority of passengers on each flight. Because of the speed of the planes, other stations will be tuned in whenever necessary to maintain proper volume for all receivers.

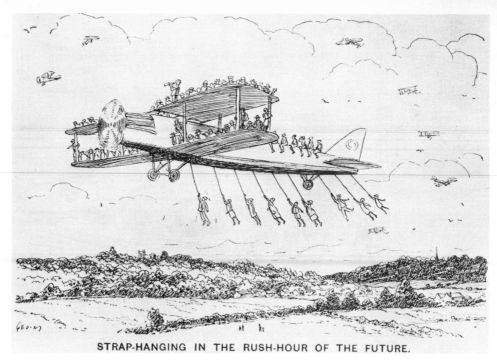

STRAP-HANGING IN THE RUSH-HOUR OF THE FUTURE.

36 Commuting Possibilities and Horrors, as seen by *Punch* in 1928

Most airlines made determined attempts to capture the businessman. In 1937, Imperial Airways, for instance, issued a special booklet, *Air Travel for Business*, and in the same year TWA made it widely known that their new coast-to-coast rates were five dollars cheaper than rail and sleeper. By this time, TWA had become fond of the businessman for what may be thought a curious reason; he gave so little trouble, compared with other kinds of passenger. The company's Passenger Relations Department had discovered that 'housewives are more critical of service than movie stars. The top-notch business executives seldom complain and are easiest to pacify when they do.'[14] One of the most interesting campaigns of this kind during the 1930s – in many ways ahead of its time – was carried out by a private British company, Crilly Airlines. A reporter noted,

For business houses and tourists special travel vouchers permitting 1,000 miles of air travel for 10 guineas are available on all Crilly inland air routes. These vouchers are transferable and exhausted by mileage only. Thus on one ticket owned by a firm representatives may travel singly or together on any number of trips within the 1,000 mile limit; or two or more friends may share the same ticket on an air holiday tour. The voucher avoids all last minute booking troubles, and in business circles is becoming steadily appreciated.

A further service calculated to be of substantial aid to the commercial man is to be introduced by Crilly Airways. This is the provision of private secretarial services in the company's offices at each airport the line touches.

In future there should be no need for a busy man to land at an airport and rush, possibly some miles, into a city to keep an appointment. He will simply telephone his friend in advance, meet him at the airport office and there transact his business with dispatch.

In existing circumstances, for instance, a traveller by Crilley [*sic*] Airways can leave Croydon at 12.20 p.m., arriving in Bristol 1.30 p.m., leave at 3 p.m., be in Leicester or Nottingham a little over an hour later, and back at Croydon in the early evening, with his business completed – a round trip of some 400 miles, costing on a travel voucher only 4 guineas.[15]

In 1930 the ever-ingenious Imperial Airways produced an original method of informing and persuading the public. This consisted of a packaged lantern-lecture, called *Wings over Empire*. There were over 100 slides, with sheets of notes to accompany them, and the whole kit could be borrowed free of charge by any individual or organisation that wanted to give the lecture. In this way, Imperial Airways publicity could be made infinitely flexible, since it was reasonably safe to assume that the lecturer knew his audience and would choose an appropriate tone and idiom. All he had to be supplied with, apart from the pictures, were reliable facts, and he received them in this form:

The Aft Saloon of the 'Scylla' – This is the aft saloon, which seats 29 passengers. It is wider than a railway carriage. There are comfortably padded chairs and big windows – tables – electric light – luggage racks – ventilating apparatus – it is quiet enough for you to talk in your ordinary voice.

This was certainly a cheap form of publicity, but its target was inevitably vague and uncertain. The lantern-lecture audiences may possibly have contained a few potential passengers for London–Paris, but it is unlikely that much business for London–Capetown would have resulted. The general idea that Imperial Airways was progressive, reliable and comfortable probably got across, however, and conditioning of this kind may well have done quite a lot of good in the long run. Anything which might help to fill a few of the second 50 per cent. of the seats was worth trying.

Standards on the pre-war long-distance routes

THE FIRST long-distance international service was planned and operated by KLM. On 12 September 1929, after a number of mail and proving flights, lasting from 1924 to 1928, KLM inaugurated a fortnightly experimental service from Amsterdam to Djakarta, in Indonesia, using the three-engined Fokker F.VVb. Until 1940 this was the longest scheduled air route in the world, 9,000 miles. The aircraft arrived at Djakarta after a flight of twelve days, via Istanbul, Baghdad, Karachi, Calcutta and Bangkok. There were no reliable maps of the route, no weather

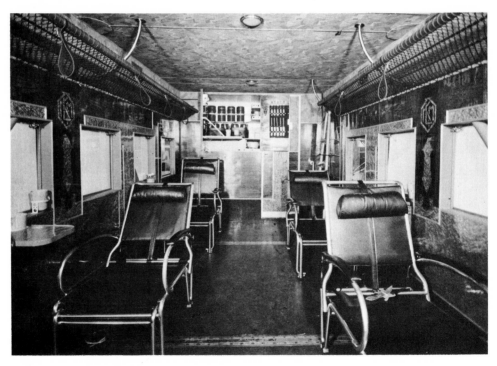

37 Room to stretch one's legs. KLM's Fokker 12, c. 1935

reports, no radio stations, no night-lighting and no hangars; fuel had to be kept in four-gallon drums. Until 1931 only mail was carried, but in October of that year Djakarta was served weekly by Fokker F.XII aircraft, which took four passengers as well, in 9 days, and 74 hours flying time. When Douglas DC-2s replaced the Fokkers in 1935, the travelling time was reduced to six days.

Mr W. H. Pilkington flew on this service in the autumn of 1935, continuing beyond Singapore to Australia and back to England in the same way, on the Imperial Airways service. He kept a detailed record of his flights.[1] For the first part of the journey there were three passengers in addition to himself: 'a pleasant middle-aged man returning to India from holiday, a man going out to visit some tea estates in Assam and returning a week later, and a man of 68 going to see his daughter in Singapore'. The crew consisted of a Captain, First Officer, Wireless Officer and Steward-Mechanic. The plane, a DC-2, he found 'most beautifully quiet: it is certainly the quietest I have ever been in', and he liked the adjustable seats, which were 'far better than any deck chair on board ship'.

They spent their first night in Athens, where conditions were not all they might have been:

Our suit cases are examined most thoroughly, and we also have to show all our money. Then there is a bit of a wait, and we are offered cups of sweet black coffee. The American and I each had one, thinking it would be, like everything else, at the KLM's expense, but found it had to be paid for. I offered 6d., and the Greek waiter seemed a bit doubtful so I offered a £1 note; after some hesitation he accepted it, and was not going to give me any change at all! Finally a Greek official came to our rescue and paid the bill, which was 8 drachmas, or 3½d.

The driver of the taxi into Athens was exceptional, even for a Greek. It was pitch dark, the road was far from straight, and our lights were poor, so he simply put his hand on the horn and went as fast as the car could go.

This morning it had been cold: now at Athens it seemed real summer warmth and very stuffy. And, strange to say, mosquitoes were about. Between three and four-thirty in the morning I was wakened five times by them biting me! The hotel is a splendid one, but right on the noisiest corner in Athens, and few of us had a really good night.

In Athens he changed into what he describes as his 'travelling clothes' – shorts and an open-necked shirt. Meals, 'good and frequent', were taken during refuelling stops and after arrival each evening, but there were also in-flight refreshments, prepared by the mechanic 'on the table immediately behind my chair; the Dutch have a great fondness for smoked eels, apparently. I shall get used to this smell by the end of the journey. And if I don't I shall make liberal use of the eau-de-Cologne spray which is within reach.'

Mr Pilkington was enthusiastic about both the crew, whom he found 'very pleasant companions', and the DC-2:

Normally they seat 14, but for these long routes half the seats are removed, and actually they never take more than six passengers. You have a comfortable chair, adjustable to any angle, with a pillow and leg rest. You have a small collapsible table and an ample rack above your head for keeping oddments. The KLM give you two very good suitcases, which fit into handy racks within reach.

The ventilation – always an important point – is very good, so that even the smell of smoked eels goes out at the back at once. You each have two forced air ventilators which are very welcome in the heat. There is also a thermostatic heating system – steam, heated by the exhaust, and switched on and off at certain temperatures. How necessary all this is, is plain when you realise that there may be a range of temperatures of considerably over 100° outside on one day. The biggest range of temperatures in 24 hours in England on the ground is about 35°, and normally it does not exceed 20°.

The continuation of the flight from Singapore was in a D.H.86 biplane, which had accommodation for six passengers, although on this occasion there were only three, and a crew of two, a Captain and a First Officer, who was also the radio operator.

At Rambang, on the island of Lombok, accommodation was provided at a resthouse:

This is the first night that we have spent away from a first-class hotel in a large city – actually the resthouse is just beyond the little town of Şelong and seems secluded. As it was dark before we arrived and when we left, I haven't much idea of the surroundings, but it was a Government resthouse with two or three bedrooms, one sitting-room, and across a sort of courtyard the bathroom. In the Tropics the bathroom is the place you make for immediately, as the constant changes of temperature arising from flying so high make you even stickier than if you have been on the ground all day. This bathroom I found a little difficult to understand at first, but apparently it is the standard Dutch East Indies type, found even in the best hotels. In a large room there is a sort of trough in one corner. This you fill with cold water (it never is really cold, and you never want anything hotter) and then take the soap in one hand and a kind of saucepan in the other; standing in the middle of the floor you ladle the water over yourself continually until you are finished. You never get into the trough itself, and therefore never have the lazy rest that we Europeans think is the chief joy of a bath. But it does all that is necessary.

The ground engineer had brought the food with him from Sourabaya. At these resthouses food is not normally provided by the landlord, and visitors are expected to bring their own. Probably the ordinary guests on an island like Lombok are very few and far between.

Immediately after our supper – delightful because of its comparatively picnic nature – we went to bed, and had a splendid cool and comfortable night under our mosquito nets. With the absence of luxuries such as electric light and hot and cold water, it reminded me of inns in the English lakes or on a walking tour.

In Brisbane, at the end of his journey, Mr Pilkington reckoned he had travelled 12,516 miles, been in the air for 4,959 minutes and landed 35 times since leaving

Amsterdam. For the flight back, he was able to benefit from his experiences going out:

I've got my luggage still lighter this time – about 55 lbs. altogether. And as Qantas have no objection to my taking out all my books and carrying them under my arm when my suit cases are being weighed, I have only got 11 lbs. on which to pay excess. On the Dutch part of the journey, when they allow 45 lbs. free, I shall probably not have to pay anything.

During the early days of the service there had been complaints about the charges made for baggage and some concessions were made.

As many passengers objected to the rates charged for personal effects, K.L.M. decided that besides the 15 kilogrammes allowed free of charge, the first additional 15 kilogrammes should be carried at 50% of the freight rate. All passengers travelling from one terminal point to another are given two suit-cases free of charge, one designed to fit below and the other slightly behind the armchair seats. These suitcases remain passengers' property, and the system has caught on.[2]

38 1932. Airport transport at Siem-Reop, Cambodia, on Saigon–Paris flight

In Australia Mr Pilkington bought a thermometer, to measure the cabin temperatures en route. With its aid, he was able to establish that at one stop in North Australia 'the temperature rose 16° in the four minutes we were on the ground'. A little further on, with the temperature 96° on the ground, they had 'good sausage rolls' for lunch. The combination of the heat and the sausage rolls did Mr Pilkington no good, and, to settle his stomach milk was taken on board at Rambang, together with 'a hamper lunch – hot omelettes and macaroni, hot peas and salmon, tinned fruit and mineral waters. Even my appetite revived at the sight. We ate whilst flying high over Bali.'

Over the Persian Gulf he noticed that 'there are five passengers in this plane, and every one of them is reading one of my books – no one else has come with sufficient literature to get them even as far as Baghdad'.

Back in England and on the train from Euston to Liverpool, Mr Pilkington occupied himself by making some comparisons between air and train travel. KLM and Imperial Airways had good reason to be pleased.

The first thing that strikes me is the noise of this train, compared with the planes. Not only is it more noisy, but the noise is so variable that it is much more noticeable.

The next thing is the unsteadiness—my cup of tea has spilt itself and I can't read my own writing – what I wrote while up in the air was occasionally legible even to others.

Then I can't see anything from here; the windows are steamed over, but when I wipe one I find the smoke from the engine obliterating the view, or else we are in a tunnel or a cutting.

It certainly isn't as comfortable – I can put my feet up on a newspaper on the opposite seat, but I still have an almost upright back to the seat; the carriage is badly ventilated and no one has ever claimed for train travel that it is clean!

And now, as a climax, I find that even though it is allowed an hour extra on Sundays, this train is half-an-hour late at Lime Street.

So the only possible conclusion is that air has all the advantages over rail or boat, and if ever I had to go again I should certainly go the same way.

Mr Pilkington's views on the Far East service were shared by another traveller during 1935.

The times of arrival were also reasonable, between five and six in the afternoon, and at the end of each day there were cars waiting to take us to good comfortable hotels – the hotels at Medan, Jodhpur and Athens were even surprising in their comfort. At every intermediate landing something pleasant was prepared for us, a well-laid table provided, and if any objection is to be made it is that we were offered in fact too much to eat. This can only adversely affect the loading capacity of the aircraft, for it was not merely a question of the early snacks, breakfasts, luncheons and afternoon teas, but on board we were continually offered tea, coffee or beef-tea with sandwiches and biscuits. It is remarkable how one's appetite increases; presumably it is due to the change of climate, as a result not only of the horizontal but also of the vertical changes in the position of the machine.

This new type of aircraft has its best performance at altitudes of 10,000–12,000 feet, at which height, when one is wearing tropical clothing, while on the ground the mercury is registering 110 and 120° F, it is very welcome to feel that the heating of the Fokker/Douglas works so well and to find that rugs are provided on board.

The Douglas chairs, with extensions, can be transformed into veritable couches; there is so much leg room that at the foot-end two suit-cases can be placed on end, one behind the other, without interfering with the chair in front. High up in the air, it is cool and well-ventilated and everyone sleeps or reads or nibbles at something and a few of those people who are always so precise, write notes in their pocket books immediately after the departure, presumably the time they left and how much they have spent, but by the third day most of them cease to do even this.

One of the pleasant things I noticed on this flight, besides the easy chairs, was the absence of noise in the cabin. The engine hum is certainly heard, but it is not annoying and I could easily converse with my fellow passengers and there was no need to plug up my ears with cotton wool. I think that what hitherto was most trying on long journeys by air was the noise and the vibration. With the Fokker/Douglas there was none of this, and that is why after even the longest day's flight I really felt quite fresh and ready to take a look round the town from the ground floor instead of viewing it from 10,000 feet up.[3]

Once the routes to Africa and the Far East were established, it became possible for children at boarding school in England to rejoin their parents for the holidays, a practice which is common enough nowadays, but was fairly rare even as late as 1939. In 1938 a girl of ten, now Mrs Constance Halford-Thompson,[4] flew from Amsterdam to visit her parents in India. She was the first unaccompanied child passenger to be taken by KLM on this route and, as a special favour, she was allowed to sit in the cockpit with the pilot. She remembers the steward telling the passengers that if anyone needed oxygen they should ask for it. When she asked, perfectly reasonably, how she would know if she needed it, the steward said a headache was the warning sign. At the first opportunity, therefore, she naturally claimed she had a headache, but when the mask was over her face and she breathed in oxygen she began to feel sick and decided her curiosity was satisfied.

On this trip all the other passengers, she recalls, were 'tough American oil-drillers'. They were very kind to her and took her on a sight-seeing trip around Athens. Some of her experiences were not so pleasant. The 5 am starts often found her very sleepy and in Basra, when dinner was eaten late and outdoors, it was hot and rather dark, so that she was unable to see what she was eating.

For people going back on leave, the new air services were a great boon. In 1935 Mr S. C. Isaacs,[5] a lawyer working in India, flew from Calcutta to London in three days, with night-stops only at Karachi and Cairo. The return ticket cost £180, which compared favourably with the first-class fare by sea. Most Anglo-Indians, however, welcomed the long sea voyage as a holiday, and since the usual

39 London–Karachi passenger ticket, 1939

40 (*opposite*) Passenger list and seating-plan

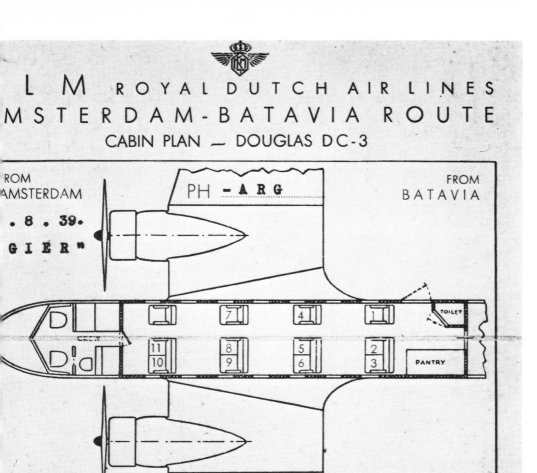

L M ROYAL DUTCH AIR LINES
MSTERDAM-BATAVIA ROUTE
CABIN PLAN — DOUGLAS DC-3

FROM AMSTERDAM

FROM BATAVIA

PH - ARG

. 8 . 39.
GIER "

r. Rasmussen	Bangkok	
r. von Guerard	Medan	
r. von Guerard	Medan	
r. Derendsen	Batavia	
r. Lamson	Karachi	
r. Lewis Crider	Karachi	

7	Miss. Tarbeur	Karachi
8	Mr. Johns	Karachi
9	Mr. Richards	Karachi
10		
11		

arrangement for people working in India was for long periods of service followed by long periods of leave, the time the sea voyage took did not bother them. It was those with short leaves who welcomed the opportunity to fly.

It is curious that for some years Imperial Airways paid no attention to Delhi, despite the fact that a steadily increasing number of people wanted to travel to and from the Indian capital. The company's advice to such people was either to use the train or to try to persuade a member of the Delhi Flying Club to give them a lift from Jodhpur in one of the Club's Puss Moths.

The reminiscences of other passengers help to build up a picture of what flying to the Far East and Australia was like in the 1930s. At Sharjah, Sir Hudson Fysh remembers

. . . the plane landed on the desert and was taxied in alongside the Imperial Airways rest-house through an opening in barbed-wire entanglements which were closed tight behind it for the night. The Sheik from the village usually paid a visit; his escort had solid gold bands to their rifles. Watch-towers on the encircling hills kept sentinel and altogether it was a romantic spot.[6]

In the primitive rest-house on Lombok Island,

. . . there were about three bedrooms, each containing a huge Dutch bed into which two or even three people had to be piled when there was a good load of passengers. The usual 'Dutch wife' was of course placed down the centre of the bed and at least served to keep the occupants apart. The lavatory amenities consisted of one cubicle with two holes in the ground and a row of bottles of water, while the bath-house in the usual Dutch style had a tiled concrete water container built into a corner, out of which the bather dipped delicious ladles of cool water, refreshing in the oppressive heat.

Like the Dutch, the British saw their long-distance services as an important part of the communications network between the mother-country and the more distant parts of their empire. The Empire services of Imperial Airways ran along two main routes, India–Australia, and South Africa. For several years during the late 1920s and early 1930s both these routes were seriously handicapped by political difficulties with the Italian government, which refused to allow foreign airlines to fly over its territory, or to land or refuel at inland aerodromes. It was consequently necessary to fly passengers from London to Paris and then take them by train-sleeper to Brindisi, where the main part of the flight began.

The journey was a leisurely one, In 1933 the London–Karachi flight left on a Saturday and arrived on a Friday, with overnight stops at Athens, Gaza, Basra and Sharjah. London–Capetown left on a Wednesday and arrived ten days later on a Sunday, the stops after Brindisi being Athens, Cairo, Wadi–Halfa, Khartoum, Juba, Nairobi, Mjeya, Salisbury and Johannesburg.

On the whole, the Far-Eastern and African routes were remarkably safe and

41 First flight Kinshasa–Loana, Portuguese
East Africa, 1929. Passengers and crew

42 Interior of Fokker F.VIIA, in service
with KLM between 1925 and 1940

95

reliable during their early years, but there were occasions when it was an advantage to have strong nerves and an optimistic temperament. During a flight down the African continent in the early 'thirties in a Handley Page Hannibal biplane, a plane which Imperial Airways proudly claimed 'had never killed a single passenger,' a very seasoned traveller[7] was sitting alone in his wicker ('wicker-for-coolness') seat in the after compartment, when the seat broke adrift during a violent bout of turbulence. A young officer assured him that the terrible vibrations were 'just turbulence', but on landing it was discovered that part of the wing had broken right off. Another passenger, an American, wanted to take a photograph of the damaged wing, but the pilot dissuaded him, on the grounds that it was 'not good advertising for flying'.

Although there was no night-flying at that time, there were occasions when a plane was delayed and had to come in late. To guide it down, oil lamps would be placed on the airfield. On one memorable occasion,[8] the pilot missed the beacon lights at Hyderabad, on his way to Karachi, and when he eventually reached Karachi he admitted he had been quite lucky, because he had only half-an-hour's fuel left. Regular passengers became very conscious of this time/fuel problem and considered it one of the inevitable hazards of flying. There was an alternative method of illuminating the airfield to make landing possible. The pilot fired rockets from the plane, the explosion being quite alarming for the passengers, if they had no warning of what was about to happen.

Major Munday, who flew to London from Mpika in Northern Rhodesia on one of the early flights, gave some useful advice based on his personal experience.[9]

Passages should be booked several weeks beforehand to avoid disappointments, as inter-mediate journeys by other passengers have to be fitted in with those of passengers undertaking longer flights. Cheques for the journey, if not sent with the order for booking, should be sent as soon as possible. The Station Superintendent at Mpika as a matter of fact took my cheque on the day prior to my departure, when I was issued with my ticket and weighed for the trip.

The total weight allowed on one ticket is 100 kilos (221 lbs.). When being issued with a ticket, the weight of the passenger and the weight of the baggage is entered separately on a slip of paper attached to the book of tickets. The baggage is labelled with a number which corresponds to a number on the ticket; the baggage required on the journey is identified by means of an additional adhesive label. Weight being available, it is advisable to carry two light suitcases, one for everyday requirements and the other for kit not required on the journey, or for a change of clothes later on the journey. Passengers found no difficulty in obtaining their second piece of luggage on landing for the night when required. Otherwise the luggage labelled 'wanted on voyage' was always landed at the hotel without any identification by the passenger or worry as to whether it had been put on or off the aeroplane. This part of the organisation seemed very efficient, and there was no anxiety as to baggage over the whole of the journey.

Passengers should be at the original aerodrome of departure some two hours before scheduled time, as favourable flying conditions are taken advantage of over the whole of the flight. At each landing ground, all is done for the convenience of passengers when waiting for the departure of the aeroplane. The pilot is in sole charge of the journey and nothing should be done to delay the starting of the aeroplane each morning. His orders are every bit as important as those of the captain of the ship. In all six pilots took charge over the various stages, and all were most considerate as to the comfort and welfare of their passengers, as well as making the journey as interesting and enjoyable as possible. No body of men could have made the journey so thoroughly enjoyable.

Careful attention should be paid to clothing for the trip:

An open neck shirt is almost necessary for the hotter days. Flannel trousers are the most comfortable. The average temperature is rather the same as in a railway train. During the early mornings it can be cold and at other times of the day very hot. Windows can be opened in some of the aeroplanes, but more than often this raises a complaint from some of the other passengers. On the whole journey clothes should be worn as on a car journey with a jumper and good rain coat handy for varying temperatures of weather.

Major Munday flew on the Hercules class airliner, *City of Cape Town*, as far as Kisumu and continued by seaplane to Brindisi. By the time he reached Croydon he calculated that he had spent 'two days, six hours and seven minutes in the air, and one day, thirteen hours and fifty-three minutes in the trains, leaving five days, four hours and thirty-six minutes being spent over meals, sleeping and sight-seeing, or 25 per cent., 17·5 per cent. and 57·5 per cent. of the time respectively'.

The overnighting system continued until the outbreak of war in 1939. It was well liked by passengers, since it gave them a good rest each night and provided an opportunity, both on the ground and from the air, of seeing something of the country over which they were travelling. The sight-seeing attractions of the journey were well publicised:

Dearest Mother,
... We left Nairobi at 6.30 a.m. and arrived in Salisbury at 10.15 p.m., stopping at Moshi for breakfast, Mbeya for lunch and Broken Hill for dinner and two other intermediate stops. It was a most interesting day. Shortly after leaving Nairobi we flew low over the great game preserve and various herds of the buck, gazelle type of animal could be seen. A little later we ran into cloud and had to climb a little to get out of them, we then got some beautiful cloud effects which I photographed. In a little time the snow crested summit of Kilimanjaro (19,712 feet high) suddenly appeared out of the morning mists on our port bow, and to starboard a handsomer cone-shaped mountain, Meru (14,950 feet) rose straight from the plain. Kilimanjaro looks rather like a plum pudding after Johnny has taken a spoonful out of the top and scraped off some of the sauce.
At Moshi we had breakfast and . . . at Dodoma we came down for fuel, all was cool, clean and civilised and delightfully arranged refreshments on a snow-white table cloth

E

showed that some English woman (or at least British) was doing her bit to make the tropics better and brighter.

After leaving here we flew over some mountains which completely enclosed an enormous plateau, which is the natural habitat of lions, elephants, giraffes, zebras, gnus, gazelles, buck &c &c and buffalo. All except the lions we saw and I photographed and hope I got them in . . . At all these stops now there were nice little stations which showed the outward and visible signs of good housewives somewhere in the offing.

Dinner at Broken Hill was a lively meal and . . . the three-quarter moon just gave enough light to see things, but it was just bush country with the Zambesi river through it . . .

I got off the Amalthea at Bulawayo this morning as I'm going on to the Victoria Falls and the only way is by train so here endeth my Imperial Airways trip from London and it has been splendid. I think the Imperial Airways put up the best show I've seen for efficiency and comfort of the passenger.

Love to all,

(signed) Harry[10]

Air journeys in Africa during the 'thirties could, however, provide both the unexpected and the tedious. One man who went by flying-boat from Mombasa to Durban in 1938[11] was irritated to discover that at Durban the customs and other airport formalities took as long as the flight itself, two hours. The health authorities came aboard, and with the passengers still in their seats, sprayed the whole of the inside of the plane with insecticide.

On a subsequent flight by South African Airways from Johannesburg to Nairobi, the same passenger noticed 'a mad-cap Englishman' giving joy-rides over the

43 Ouakam, Dakar, 1928.
The Airport watchman

Victoria Falls. He took two passengers at a time, and, since they were both anxious to take photographs, he obliged by angling the plane from side to side.

After 1937 the Africa service of Imperial Airways was operated largely by flying-boats, which provided exceptionally comfortable conditions, bettered only by the German airships. They, and the attentive service they offered, are still recalled with great affection by the people who travelled in them. In the Empire flying-boats,

... the midship cabin is located behind the mail compartments, kitchen and toilets and accommodates three passengers by day and four at night. Then, further astern, comes the big promenade cabin seating eight or resting four. On the port side is a rail for elbow resting by the windows and a surprising amount of space for promenading. Leg stretching space is always welcome on long trips. Above this cabin is a loft for bedding stowage, and behind it a further cabin with six seats for daylight flying or sleeping accommodation for four. The rear wall of this cabin coincides with the farther step of the planing bottom and behind it, extending well into the stern portion of the hull, is another hold for mail, freight and baggage.

Every bunk has a little window above it with a cover flap and by each row of seats are universally mounted hot and cold air intakes and a light incorporating a switch and a bell-push for calling the steward. Little hold-alls are let into the walls at appropriate points. Light luggage racks of railway carriage design are installed to form back rests. The upholstery over the double sound-proofed walls and on the seats is mainly in a dark restful green.[12]

The Empire flying-boats offered exceptional amenities, which were greatly appreciated by passengers. There was, for instance, a smoking cabin. Mr Rupert Belleville, of White's Club, fined £10 for smoking while travelling from Paris to London in *Heracles* in 1936 (see p. 52) would have found himself without a problem if he had chosen to go to South Africa instead. The price of meals was included in the ticket and, to sort out any difficulties passengers might have, there was a Ship's Clerk on board, with his own little office. In the later Frobishers

The cabins are furnished after the luxurious style of interior decoration which makes me feel that the Flight Steward should be called Head Waiter. There are three cabins. But cabin is a mean word to give to these three areas, carpeted richly and deeply, not shaped in front but nearly square, with sofa-like double seats on either side of the through walk down the middle. The three cabins have the same floor level, and the ceiling is low, 6 ft. 2 ins. in the middle and rounded to the window lines' sides. Perhaps it is partly these lower ceilings of the Frobishers that make them still more comfortable than their big cousins, the Ensigns and the Imperial flying boats. And the dark fawn colour scheme is entirely pleasant – carpet, sofas, curtains, cloth covered ceiling and walls and all in tones of fawn. The whole job was carried out by Imperial Airways' Battersea factory and I must feel that some internationally famous interior designer must have been put to work to produce this excellent result. The semicircular bracket light fittings give an upward

44 Promenade deck on Empire flying-boat. 1938

46 (*opposite*) Boeing 314 Clipper. Cutaway of fuselage showing accommodation. 1938 onwards

45 Empire flying-boat *Corsair* on slipway at Imperial Airways base, Hythe, Kent. The Empire flying-boats flew the trunk routes to Africa, the Far East and Australia, from 1936

Boeing 314

and indirect light and are made of the same fine, almost weightless, gold-coloured dura-lumin as all the fittings. Even the notices on the walls and doors are made to agree with this very simple decoration scheme. The central heating is done by steam, just as in any modern luxury flat. But the Flight Steward's small 3 ft. 6 ins. by 3 ft. 6 ins. kitchen shames even the most modern flat. It is a perfect example for any kitchen planning expert. Here there is a place for everything and everything in its place – big thermos containers for serving hot meals, an ice chest for drinks, cutlery, linen, china, glass, cigarettes, cards, writing paper and the rest, all neatly stored away in next to no space at all.[13]

The American Clippers, used between Manila and Hong Kong in the late 1930s, aimed at rather more functional style, with cool decorations in silver and pale green and a self-service pantry equipped with an ice-box, water-taps and plastic cups, cotton-wool for ear plugs, bags for air-sickness and fresh-air tubes.

A clue to the very high standard of attention is to be found in an Imperial Airways' booklet published in 1938. Outlining the duties of the steward, it says

He can supply you at any time during your journey with the following articles:
(a) Free of charge. Cocoa, coffee, chocolate, Bovril, sandwiches, cocktail snacks, biscuits, fresh fruit, pencils, notepaper, postcards, booklets descriptive of the route and maps, guides to night stops, aspirin, smelling salts, eau de Cologne; Eno's Fruit Salts, cotton wool, barley sugar, saccharine, Glucose D, air-sickness tablets, soap and towels.
(b) On sale. Cigarettes (Virginia, Turkish and Egyptian), alcoholic and non-alcoholic beverages and mineral waters.
(c) Available for use on journey free of charge. Playing cards, crossword puzzles, jigsaw puzzles, books, papers, children's magazines and games, sun glasses.

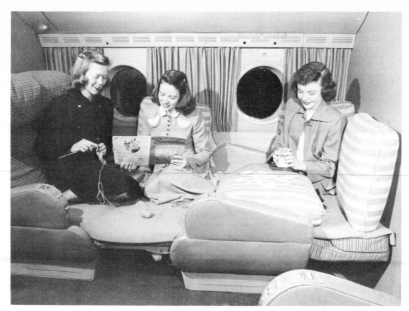

47 Forward stateroom in Boeing 314 Clipper,
showing seats folded down to make a bed

48 Cabin interior of Boeing 314 Clipper

It should be mentioned, perhaps, that throughout the 1930s the cabin staff on long-distance flights were always men. Air France employed stewardesses in 1931 and KLM in 1935 – the more conservative Imperial Airways would have none of them – but only on the shorter services. This was mainly to avoid possible complications during overnight stops, complications which became a more-or-less accepted reality after 1945. There could, however, be difficulties even with stewards. On one occasion a British passenger who had travelled by KLM from the Far East complained on arrival at Schiphol that both the co-pilot and the steward on his aircraft had been Indonesian and that, in consequence, he had been compelled to spend his evenings at the hotels and rest-houses en route in close company with people who were not Europeans. The station manager at Schiphol who received his complaint was himself Indonesian.[14]

British passengers, especially of the old imperialist type, may have presented exceptional problems, but they were rarely indifferent to food or to a comfortable sitting position. The nearer conditions in an aeroplane approached those of a good London club, the more contented they were likely to be, a fact which impressed visiting Americans, who tended to rate an aeroplane's technicalities higher than its meals.

In 1939 the well-known American aeronautical journalist, Cy Caldwell, delivered his opinions about this.

The English air traveller demands four things: comfort, tobacco, drink, food. Imperial Airways provides all four, with superlatively fine service, not only on the Paris run but also on the Short Empire boats, on one of which I later flew from Rome to Southampton. As we took off from Croydon the steward handed around wine lists; everybody ignored them and ordered Scotch and soda or bottled ale – wines are only for banquets, or foreigners. I ministered to my bronchial affliction with Scotch and soda, but what helped most was the sight of the sun, the first glimpse in two weeks, as we came out of a solid overcast about mid-channel. By this time hardy Britons were eating Consommé Julienne, fricassée of chicken, roast fillet of veal, ham and egg salad, and cheese, Gorgonzola, Cheddar or Cheshire. . . . The stewards move with the grace and speed of panthers – the only things I saw in England that moved faster were Spitfires and Hurricanes. In slightly less than an hour and a half everyone had been filled up with something, the dishes and glasses were whisked away, nearly everyone was smoking and we were gliding down through another dismal overcast to Le Bourget. I was sorry to get out; it had been like sitting in a comfortable friendly club. It is the English genius for being human and understanding with air travellers that makes Imperial Airways one of the best liked services in the world. This is not only my impression; several other travellers, mostly Americans, also felt the same way.[15]

However much passengers appreciated the service they received, they were officially forbidden to tip the stewards, or, indeed, any other member of the airline staff. This, from the beginning, was the great difference between travelling by air and travelling by rail or boat.

Imperial Airways never missed the opportunity to provide their passengers with a news-worthy meal.

Probably the favourite national holiday in the U.S.A. is that of Thanksgiving which takes place at the end of November. An essential part of this holiday is a lunch or dinner at which turkey and cranberry sauce is served. In true American style a Thanksgiving dinner was served aboard Imperial Airways' flying boat *Cavalier* en route from New York to Bermuda on that day.[16]

Much progress had been made since October 1919, when Handley Page Transport made the first attempt at an aerial luncheon service, with baskets of sandwiches, fruit and chocolate, at 15p (3s.) a head.

The operators were well aware that, on the Eastern and the African routes, a reputation for substantial, hotel-like meals was of great importance to them. They were more likely to be complimented for this than for anything else.

Passengers making air journeys in the new *Empire* type flying boats of Imperial airways not only express their admiration for the speed and quietness in flight of these air liners, and for the spaciousness of their saloons, but they also pay warm tributes to the efficiency of their catering arrangements.

Well-equipped kitchens at air ports, and a completely fitted buffet in the flying boats, enable Imperial Airways to serve, up in the air, meals which are in their way the equal of those supplied in first class restaurants or hotels.

Here, for example, chosen at random, is a luncheon menu served the other day in the flying boat *Challenger*. It began with iced melon. Then followed roast chicken, York

49 Meal-time on an Imperial Airways 'Hermes' flight, 1937

ham and veal galantine, with tomatoes and asparagus tips. Then came fruit salad and cream, followed by Cheshire, Cheddar or cream cheese, with 'toast Imperial', assorted biscuits, crystallised fruit, coffee and liqueur brandy.

Here is a dinner menu in the *Corsair*: Paté de foie gras or grape fruit – roast chicken, ox tongue, York ham and Russian salad, green salad – peaches and sauce Melba, golden figs, Cheshire, Camembert, Kraft cheese – 'toast Imperial', biscuits, dessert and coffee.

Passengers in all the big air liners of Imperial Airways have a comprehensive wine list from which to make a choice while a feature is also made of an intriguing 'Airway' cocktail.[17]

There were those, however, even in the extremely food-conscious Imperial Airways, who gave the seat a higher priority than the meals, when it was a matter of pleasing passengers. The Traffic Manager of Imperial Airways, Mr D. H. Handover, put this very well:

I think anyone asked to remember the last journey he made, whether it was by train, by boat, by car or by aeroplane, will find that the abiding impression which remained was not the speed at which it was accomplished but whether it was comfortable. Making passengers comfortable in the air is a task to which many small details contribute. What are needed are space, fresh air, good ventilation, heating, good catering, an attentive steward service and, essentially, comfortable seating arrangements. By sea an outside room with bath is demanded, but by air the passenger's time is spent chiefly seated in a chair and, depending upon his mood, that chair must enable him to sit upright when taking his meals, or to loll back in luxurious comfort to read, and in it he must be able to recline or doze or sleep. All this must his chair fulfil, and that independently of his fellow passenger, who may require his chair to do quite the opposite and at the same time. Imperial Airways has recently completed a chair of its own invention which is fitted as standard to the new flying-boats and landplanes. Its comfort and adjustability show a marked improvement on anything of its kind yet in use; moreover, its weight is only 18 lbs. – a vital factor from the aircraft operator's point of view.[18]

Imperial Airways were extremely proud of this chair. They had researched it themselves, patented it[19] and named it the Imperial Airways Adjustable Chair. It was manufactured under licence by Accles and Pollock and later, in 1938, by Junkers in Germany. Many thousands of travellers to Africa and the East had reason to be grateful for it.

It is instructive and humbling to contrast the remarkable attention paid to the comfort of passengers who belonged to the European and American business and social élite and who were in a position to pay or have paid for them fares of the order of £225 to Durban or £288 to Brisbane – huge sums if one translates them into today's money values – with the rough and ready treatment meted out to more ordinary people in other parts of the world. But the international companies at least were sensitive to complaints and did what they could to bring about improvements. One wonders what the consequences were of a letter[20] written in 1933 by an American lady to the representative of American Express in Yokohama, after a not very comfortable flight from Japan to Manchuria. She had been very cold.

In cool weather in Imp. Air-Ways--(Crayden [*sic*], London) they give us each a traveling rug when seated. Now, this matter must be organized and as you are Amexco--guess it's up to you! All over the world--we *must* have rugs. Yesterday my guide bought me one (a light brown bed blanket) in Autung, Manchuria--across the border from air-drome for hotel ('Auto Hotel)'. I put the paper off the blanket across the front of me under my coat, and the blanket I sat in and put my hands into it. Under my coat, in the back, I had put the 'Jap silk wadding' that Mrs. Seko gave me, to get home comfortably last Saturday Nite. So I rode comfortably the last 1½ hours, that is on this morning lap.

Why can't the Airway companies have traveling rugs for hire? Say 25¢ (1 Y/ R.M. etc). (If they don't want to supply them for the journey). They could also have clean (and clean looking) gauntlet mittens for us, as I could not keep the draught out from my wrists. Fortunately, I had my overshoes but still I would have welcomed a large paper sort of shopping bag to have put my feet into as they were very cold. Others were cold also. (They use these in America in motoring).

Now in your own booklets, in referring to air going--(unless it be in hottest climes and seasons) could suggest that for complete comfort it is well to put a muffler on, extra pair of stockings and gloves, and sit in a rug. If one does this, then the flight is so very much more enjoyable, but rugs should really be supplied.

This unfortunate passenger was well informed about the rugs provided by the major airlines. The necessity for them passed, however, and by 1938 it was possible to tell ladies contemplating a journey by air,

There is no need to wrap yourself up. All aeroplanes are heated and air conditioned. If you do feel the need for a rug, rugs are provided – and on Empire routes foot muffs too.

These air liners are so spacious that there is plenty of room for passengers to walk about; the Imperial flying boats have a promenade deck. And there is no need to worry about noise, for the walls are insulated, allowing conversation to be carried on in a normal voice.

If the ears should get that 'full' feeling as they do sometimes when climbing high mountains, this can be stopped by swallowing hard or yawning several times or holding the nose and blowing with mouth closed.[21]

That 'full' feeling had to be suffered for a few more years, until pressurised cabins became standard. During the first quarter of a century of air travel, however, it was as normal as soot and smuts were to passengers in a steam-hauled train and a boiling radiator to a pioneering motorist.

50 American aircraft on British cigarette-cards – nineteen-thirties

PLAYER'S CIGARETTES

EASTERN AIRLINES: DOUGLAS D.C.2

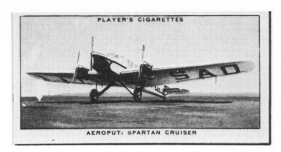

PLAYER'S CIGARETTES

AEROPUT: SPARTAN CRUISER

PLAYER'S CIGARETTES

EASTERN AIRLINES: LOCKHEED "ELECTRA"

PLAYER'S CIGARETTES

AMERICAN AIRLINES: DOUGLAS D.S.T.

PLAYER'S CIGARETTES

NORTHWEST AIRLINES: LOCKHEED "ELECTRA"

PLAYER'S CIGARETTES

BRANIFF AIRWAYS: LOCKHEED "ELECTRA"

PLAYER'S CIGARETTES

PAN AMERICAN AIRWAYS: GLENN MARTIN 130 FLYING-BOAT "CHINA CLIPPER"

PLAYER'S CIGARETTES

CENTRAL AIRLINES: STINSON "A"

PLAYER'S CIGARETTES

PAN AMERICAN AIRWAYS: MAIN AISLE, "CLIPPER" CLASS FLYING-BOAT

PLAYER'S CIGARETTES

DELTA AIRLINES: LOCKHEED "ELECTRA"

51 The ladies' powder room on board an Imperial Airways 'Hermes'

6

The war years

SOME AIRLINES did much better than others from the 1939–45 war, but none found themselves without considerable problems and some, such as Lufthansa and KLM, were virtually obliterated. Taking a world view, however, the war achieved three things, so far as passenger transport was concerned. It brought about great technical advances in the design and operation of aircraft, it accustomed millions of people to a very basic kind of air travel and it killed certain pre-war assumptions fairly completely.

One of these assumptions was that air travel would become increasingly more comfortable and more gracious. How unreal this forecast eventually became can be seen by studying an article[1] written towards the end of 1939 by Mr Howard Ketcham, the President of Howard Ketcham, Inc., a well-known American company specialising in interior design. Mr Ketcham had been responsible for the interiors of a number of large airliners, including the tri-motor Fords and, at the time the article was published, he was working on designs for United Air Lines' new DC-4s. These aimed at 'commodious luxury', and his sketches make a modern reader gasp. The lounges he envisaged – the war put a stop to their realisation – were as spacious as those of a West End club, with no sign of seating in rows or crowding of any kind. They were based on the belief that the passenger should be made at least as comfortable as in a large car or in a Pullman train. 'Pullman travel', Mr Ketcham pointed out, 'currently attracts about twenty times that of air traffic' and went on to say that passengers would only be won over from the railways by being provided with conditions better than those to be found in a Pullman car. The objective was 'gracious cabins', with armchairs facing port-holes, exactly as on a ship. 'Chairs by the windows are located so that the passenger is constantly presented with the spectacle of a fleeting terrain below without having to crane his neck.'

In the styling of this airliner, various means are employed to avoid the monotony inevitable where a long row of seats is required. Effective in this respect is the replacement of the usual vestibule with a commodious 'cluby' lounge. The immediate impression gained upon entering the ship is one of luxury, space and ease hitherto not experienced by the air traveler.

52 1970. Interior of Hugh ('Playboy') Hefner's private aircraft, *The Big Bunny*. This aeroplane, with its ample space and luxurious equipment, brings reality into the dreams of pre-war aircraft designers. They, however, saw 'Big Bunny' comfort as the future norm for ordinary airline passengers, not as the exclusive privilege of millionaires.

In flight, this lounge serves as a reception center; thus, the space is put to double purpose. There is ample room to play games, listen to music or engage in amicable conversation. Here tea or cocktails can be readily served. There is a large circular table which can be removed easily while the passengers are boarding or disembarking. On the left of the entrance is an end table containing a typewriter, stationery and other writing equipment for the passengers' use. The folding chair accompanying the table may be housed within it when it is not being used.

The aft portion of the lounge may be curtained for use as a private compartment in the event there is need for such a facility.

In another arrangement, which was suggested as an alternative scheme, the elimination of one day seat would allow a rearrangement of the layout so that a larger lounge space could be located midship. By adopting this plan the monotony from the procession of identical seats is eliminated and the entire aeroplane acquired a more interesting club-like atmosphere.

The asymmetrical arrangement thus achieved provides greater opportunity to inject interesting color effects. Its central location makes it conveniently accessible from all parts of the passenger cabin.

The reality, as post-war travellers soon came to realise, was to be quite different, with all dreams of space gone and passengers packed tightly together in rows, like the audience in the cheaper seats at a theatre and with about the same amount of room. The pre-war luxury was quietly buried, a victim of increased speed and of the operating costs of the 1950s.

To begin with, however, the worst thing the airlines had to cope with, apart from the requisitioning of their aircraft and the closing of many of their routes, was the failure of the typical pre-war passenger to realise there was a war on. In an attempt to explain the situation, Imperial Airways issued a brochure called *Flying in Wartime*. It began by posing some typical questions:

Why did I have so much trouble getting a seat? Why, even after I had booked, could they never be certain that I should get away? Why did I have to be there so long before we started and then hang about for hours? Why do they make such a fuss about passports and customs? Why do they fly so low? Why can't they tell me even now when we are going to arrive anywhere? . . .

These are some of the questions you may be asking yourself as you set out to fly across Europe in wartime.

An attempt was then made to supply convincing answers:

British and French Authorities have absolute power in wartime to commandeer accommodation on any plane at any time right up to the moment of its departure. They are as sparing as possible in exercising this right, but ordinary passengers are bound to be displaced from time to time. It is unnecessary to point out that such inconvenience is unavoidable in the interest of the Allied Cause. . . .

Civil planes must fly at a specified height and not in cloud. This means that unless the clouds are above 1000 feet we cannot fly at all, although it may be perfectly clear on the earth. This leads to many delays – sometimes of 24 hours or more. Even if we can fly, we may not be able to do so at a height of more than 1500 or 2000 feet. Flying is frequently uncomfortable at such levels, due to disturbed air so near the ground. The speed of the plane is also reduced and the journey therefore takes longer.

As one person reflected: 'The war-time traveller either ages rapidly with chronic irritation or develops a philosophic outlook.'[2] This particular traveller had crossed the Atlantic from Newfoundland a few months earlier in a Liberator bomber. His account of the journey does not suggest comfort.

We had to wait while a large number of bags were put on board. We could see that most of them went into the nose of the machine. In the meantime, Mr. M. told me that he had not been up in a plane before and that he had been recommended to chew gum during the ascents and descents. I confessed that I too had not been up in a plane before, so he gave me some of his chewing gum. Mr. P., however, had flown across the Pacific from the Dutch East Indies a few weeks previously. We regarded him as an experienced traveller. Eventually we followed the crew into the plane; Mr. J., the senior M.A.P. official, wished us a comfortable journey. He asked me to hand the flying suit to the Reception Officer at our destination, and reminded me that he would appreciate a note giving my opinion of its suitability. In due course I did both.

We entered the plane through a small opening almost in the bottom of the fuselage, the door opening downwards and bearing steps on its inner side. We found ourselves in a high compartment which is perhaps best described as the main well of the machine. To the right were steps up to the tail compartment, while to the left was a passage way to the foreward part of the machine. There were also some steps up to the wireless operator's cabin. We were undecided where to go until the wireless operator told us that the captain preferred passengers to be in the bomb bay while the plane was taking off. So we moved forward into the next compartment. Our eyes were not accustomed to the darkness and we could see practically nothing. Very gingerly, I sat down on something; it turned out to be a box. One of the Dutchmen sat beside me and the other sat on the floor. We started to chew gum. The plane was running across the field; we felt it turn two or three times. It stopped for a few minutes and then there was a mighty roar. I could see a little now and I looked at my watch. The time was just 8.30 a.m. Eastern Standard Time. This was the time of departure mentioned to us that morning by Mr. H., so things were proceeding according to plan. I gripped two of the struts in the centre of the compartment and hearing one of my companions say 'Brace yourself', I pressed my feet on a bag opposite. All sorts of whines and scraping noises, and the sound of pumps, could be heard just forward of us. There was a steadily increasing rush of air. Looking along the inside of the plane, I saw the tail come up. I chewed vigorously. We began to move more smoothly and soon we were obviously off the ground. We remained seated for about ten minutes. I looked around the walls of the compartment; there were so many gadgets and groups of leads that the place must have been an electrician's paradise. There were numerous wires, too, running along sets of pulleys.[3]

The first stage of the journey was to the Air Ferry Terminal, where everyone disembarked and prepared for the main crossing.

This time I sat on some piled-up parachutes, all in bags closed with Zipp fasteners; M. now had the box of drugs, while P. sat on the floor. When the plane moved we guessed that it was going to the corner of the field from which we had seen the Lockheed-Hudson take off, and we felt it turn round into the wind. Without any delay the engines accelerated· and we took off. It was 4.25 p.m. E.S.T. I had been told in the hotel that these planes leave the ground and travel a mile or more at a height of only a few feet before soaring upwards. When we walked out into the well we saw that the oxygen masks had been put out. These masks were really rubber nosebags, with head straps similar to those of a civilian respirator; they are also fitted with a long rubber supply tube. There were several oxygen cylinders strapped together in one corner of the well and from these lengths of metal tubing led to a number of wall points, probably three dozen in all, in different parts of the plane. Each point consisted of a gauge, a valve and a nozzle. The gauge was graduated in thousands of feet of altitude; the valve could be turned to increase the flow of oxygen through the gauge to agree with the altitude value given out by the captain. The maximum altitude shewn on the gauge was 30,000 feet. In the United States Air Force it is customary for oxygen to be taken when the altitude exceeds 15,000 feet. The long rubber lead would permit of considerable freedom of movement and presumably one could detach the lead from one point, attach it to the next vacant one and so move about the plane.

I climbed up and looked out of a window. We were fairly high up and above two layers of occasional clouds. Before long I could see the coastline. As we passed over it, the plane jolted two or three times. These jolts would have passed unnoticed in a railway train, but were most apparent here because so far our flight had been so smooth. From the position in which I was standing I could see both wing tips through windows on opposite sides of the plane. Both tips were steady; perhaps there was a slight regular up and down motion, but it was indeed slight, the amplitude being no more than an inch or two and negligible on that great wing span.

I sat down beside the wireless operator, on the step of his cabin. He was sitting in a swivel chair, with panels of instruments on tables on three sides of him. The general colour scheme of his cabin was green, the carpet on the floor matching. He was occupied in exchanging frequent weather reports.

This day, I learnt later, had been an exceedingly hot one in Canada. But here, ten thousand feet over the Atlantic and two hours after leaving Newfoundland, I put on an extra pair of socks and also my overcoat. I was wearing a waistcoat, too, for the first time since April 15th. An hour later the wireless operator put on his bearskin flying suit and a pair of fleece-lined boots. That was the moment for which I had been waiting. I took off my overcoat and donned my flying trousers. The bottoms were closed and shoe-shaped, so that my feet were entirely enclosed in fleece and padding. I struggled into the upper garment. I found that there was one large kangaroo-like pocket in the front. The wireless operator became quite cheerful and now smiled frequently. I sat up on one of the wide, upholstered ledges behind his cabin and in this position I could see, through one of the windows, two layers of cloud above the sea. Looking down through gaps in the layers I thought I could see a convoy, but we passed over the clouds so quickly that I could not make a second observation to verify the first.

We had supper. Packets of sandwiches and seven large thermos flasks had been put on board at the flying field in Newfoundland. The mechanic came for three of the flasks and some of the sandwiches and carried them forward. The wireless operator had his supper upstairs in his cabin. The three passengers sat on the ledges. The two Dutchmen had brought emergency rations with them; M. carried their sandwiches. We had plenty of food. I poured out the coffee for the three of us, standing the cups on one of the wide ledges. I am quite sure that I did not spill a drop and I know that I filled the cups more than I would in a railway dining car. That is a testimony to the smoothness of the flight.

The sun was setting. P. went off to sleep on the mattress in the tail. M. decided to go into the bomb compartment, where there was another mattress. There was also a third mattress there, but I climbed back again to the upholstered ledge. I wanted to be near a window. Sitting up with two pillows behind me, I watched the sunset. Later I settled down and pulled my raincoat over me. Shortly afterwards the wireless operator climbed down to locate a suspected leak in his oxygen apparatus. He was not wearing his mask, but thought that he could hear the sound of gas escaping along the tube. We checked the valves and verified that there was adequate pressure in his cylinder. He seemed satisfied and I climbed back to my ledge. M. came out of the bomb compartment to look for P's contribution to their emergency rations. He was feeling the cold. He wore his overcoat, with a blanket wrapped round his waist beneath it. He envied me my flying suit. I was sufficiently warm and gave him my overcoat, which I had tossed on to some parachutes on an opposite ledge. He returned to his mattress. P. was apparently asleep; he had wisely brought two blankets with him, and in the dim light from the wireless operator's cabin I could see only his nose. I pulled my hood about my face because my cheeks were cold, put on my gloves, drew my raincoat over me and tucked my hands into the kangaroo pocket. I slept for an hour or two and then noticed faint streaks of light in the sky. My watch indicated about 10.30 p.m. I watched the red orb of the sun rise between the two engines on the port wing. It seemed strange to see a dawn at 11 p.m., but my watch was still on Canadian Eastern Standard Time.

The clouds below us seemed solid, like ice floes with numerous crevasses. At times I could see lower layers down these crevasses and catch occasional glimpses of the sea.

At about three hours after the dawn I saw mountains through gaps in the clouds. The clouds were now thinning out and I could see a ragged coastline and islands. Then I saw a barrage balloon gleaming in the sunshine, the lower end of its cable passing down into a cloud. Shortly afterwards I saw several others lower down and almost beneath us. We turned in a large sweep and cut into the clouds. Soon I saw, down below, a landing ground; we circled above it, losing height. From my window I saw the retractable wheel dropped from its resting place in the wing. I called to P, and we climbed down into the bomb bay ready for the descent. We chewed gum vigorously and gripped the struts as before. I chewed more vigorously than ever because my ears had been singing for half-an-hour after stepping out in Newfoundland. I realise now that it is frequent swallowing and not the action of chewing which relieves the air pressure in the inner ear. However, I chewed vigorously, with the result that later on I had not only the singing in my ears but also aching jaws.

We did not get the bump we were expecting; the machine continued flying. The mechanic hurried past us and went up into the tail. After a few minutes he went forward again, but returned after another short interval. In passing us this time he told us that the retractable wheel on the starboard side was sticking and would not drop. All this happened so quickly that we hadn't time to remember to be nervous. I remarked that I was glad I had taken off my flying suit shortly after dawn. I am sure that if I had come down in that flying suit I should have been mistaken for a certain colleague of a notorious parachute jumper, who is now safely locked away. In a matter of seconds everything seemed to be all right. We lost height rapidly, landed and came to a standstill. When I stepped out on Scottish soil I looked at my watch. The time was 2.20 a.m. We had been flying for 9 hours 55 minutes in this second hop of two thousand two hundred miles over the Atlantic Ocean.

This was not flying as Imperial Airways or their passengers had understood it, but it allowed the distance to be covered quickly and probably with rather less danger than by sea.

At the beginning of the Second World War, the United States had seven land aircraft that could fly over the ocean.[4] TWA owned five of them, the new Stratoliners. Bases were set up in South America and Africa for South Atlantic operations. The two big American airlines, Pan American and TWA, gained a great deal of experience of transatlantic flying during the war years and the first of them continued to operate an extensive passenger network in South America. In general, commercial flying was much more normal in America, Africa and Australia during the war than it was in Europe, where nothing like the usual services were maintained even within the great area controlled by the Germans.

KLM adapted itself to the war-time situation in a remarkably resourceful and dogged way. Soon after the outbreak of war in 1939 the company had to suspend its domestic services in the Netherlands and its whole European network, with the exception of some services to Scandinavia, Belgium and Great Britain. These remaining services also came to an end after the invasion of the Netherlands in May 1940.

Every effort was made to keep the service to Djakarta going. With Amsterdam no longer available, the Western terminal became first Naples and then Tel Aviv, until the service stopped altogether in February 1942, owing to the occupation of Indonesia by the Japanese. In August 1940 KLM started a service between Bristol and Lisbon, on a charter for BOAC. This service was maintained throughout the war, frequently under very difficult circumstances, and it was even extended to Gibraltar.

What travelling on the England–Lisbon service meant has been described by a businessman who flew this way in 1942. They departed from Bristol, but it took several attempts before Lisbon was eventually reached:

There were five passengers and three of the crew, and it took two hours for the eight of us to be taken carefully through all the important formalities of Customs, immigration, censorship, currency permits, and so on. The Immigration Authorities nowadays require to be satisfied of your bona-fides and of your reasons for travelling before they will let you out of the country – particularly in the direction of Lisbon, the last link with Europe.

The Censorship Authorities are even more particular; travellers are expected to get their papers and printed matter examined and sealed up several days before leaving, but the examination of the few that had accumulated since my first disappointment took quite a long time to scrutinise, and questions were asked about several of them. As for money, a permit is required to take out more than £10, and I had been able to obtain a permit for £25, which was all liable to be needed if I were held up anywhere on the way. During all this two hours we were kept in a cold little room about ten feet square, with a military guard, but eventually everything was ready, and we boarded a camouflaged ....[5] aeroplane. When Holland was invaded 1st May the Dutch managed to save a large part of their fine fleet of civil aircraft from the clutches of the Germans, and had flown several 'planes to England, where they were now entrusted with the task of flying this service to Lisbon three times a week, with their own crews, under charter with British Overseas Airways Corporation.

We took off without incident, but the windows were blacked out and there was no sun, so that we couldn't even tell our general direction from the shadows; after 40 minutes we were surprised when we landed, and assumed it was somewhere in Cornwall, for re-fuelling, but when the door was opened we realised with great disappointment that we had come back again to our starting place. Apparently the weather off Portugal was so bad that there was no chance of going on that day – for a flight of that length without navigational aids, a pilot cannot take chances, so we had to come back to the hotel we had left about four hours earlier.[6]

They tried several times to make the flight, but each time the weather was too bad and they had to turn back again. On the eighth attempt they succeeded in reaching Lisbon.

One of the passengers was the Press Attaché from the Embassy in Lisbon.

He wanted to take home to his wife a present, so he chose some carnations and a brace of pheasants. These were clearly not up to the strain of our continual delays, so after a couple of days he gave the first brace to the soldiers at the airport, and went to the market to arrange to buy a fresh brace with the right to exchange it every day for a further one still. The brace that eventually reached Lisbon was the sixth. The carnations lasted better, and it was only the second bunch that eventually made the journey.

Having taken off for the eighth time,

. . . after two hours the shutters were taken down, and we were able to scan the grey ocean below in the hopes of seeing some ships. But not a ship did we see, and no land until we were off the coast of Spain several hours later. The long flight was really quite uneventful, and late in the afternoon we got to Cintra, Lisbon's airport, about 20 miles from the city.

There we landed in our drab, camouflaged 'plane, and drew up alongside the gleaming silver German 'plane that had arrived a few minutes previously. The wife of our press attaché was there to meet him, and told how she had come out day after day in the hope that the 'plane was coming, and every day this gleaming German monster ostentatiously arrived to time – having, of course, no difficulties to encounter, travelling over friendly or neutral territory the whole way, with regular stops at Strasbourg, Lyons, Barcelona and Madrid, and plenty of emergency landing grounds as well. We, of course, had come well over 1,000 miles with always the possibility of meeting enemy 'planes, with no accurate information about the weather en route, unable to use our radio as a navigation aid, with no intermediate landing ground except Oporto. . . .

There are many accounts of similar journeys made during the war, some in seaplanes, some in land-planes, all preceded by tedious waiting and all rather dreary and uncomfortable during the flight. War-time flying was not a gracious affair. Women very rarely travelled on these priority flights. This was, in fact, one of the strange results of the war, at least in Europe. By 1945 a very large number of men had been added to the pool of experienced air travellers, but the number of women with experience of journeys by air was no greater than in 1939. For more than six years, in Britain, as in most European countries, very few women indeed had any opportunity to fly. During that period a new generation grew up which knew nothing about the pre-war traditions of service and comfort. The airlines consequently found it quite easy to re-start their services with new, and mostly lower, standards, without any great feeling of resentment or grievance among their customers, most of whom were grateful, after the long gap, to have any kind of air service at all.

The passengers were not the only people who had forgotten the old traditions. When Mr F. C. Gillman, afterwards chief of public relations, joined the refurbished BOAC after the war, he discovered that his main task was to educate the departmental heads into accepting the strange notions that air travel had to be publicised and sold.[7] Most of them had grown up in an atmosphere of war-time security, when it was a privilege to be given a seat in an aircraft and when selling was irrelevant. Even people who had previously worked for Imperial Airways had been corrupted in this way. The non-commercial situation continued for some time after the war. The Government held priority seats on all flights and seats could be released to fare-paying passengers only with their permission. This bureaucratic millstone was difficult to shed.

One must not, however, exaggerate the bad effects of the war on civil aviation. Between 1939 and 1945 flying made great progress, in aeroplanes, in navigation systems, in flight-control and in the techniques of handling large numbers of passengers. The fact that these passengers were military personnel is of no great consequence. What is important, in view of later developments, is that they had to be fed, embarked and disembarked with the utmost speed and efficiency and that the experience of doing this was available to the airlines when the war ended.

53 How the rich fly. *Punch,* 1939

7

Flying becomes normal: Passengers as walking freight

In PRE-WAR days, recalled Mr Walter Wren,[1] 'everyone travelled *en prince*'. Stewards gave the kind of service one expected and got on first-class liners, a car was always waiting alongside the plane, porters carried baggage, everything was as it should be and flying was a pleasure.

The war and the increase in the cost, size and speed of aircraft changed the whole concept of how airlines should be run. Before the war, the majority of airline passengers were the rich and businessmen. By the 1950s, almost any aeroplane contained a complete cross-section of people[2] and the airlines were dealing in millions of passengers each year, instead of the pre-war tens or hundreds of thousands. The two types of public could not be handled in the same way. The techniques of mass transport are not the same as the techniques of élite transport, just as the Ritz is not a hamburger bar. The task of the airlines since the war has been to provide an acceptable service which is between the levels of the Ritz and the hamburger bar and this, as any caterer would admit, is not an easy thing to do. Looked at from this point of view, the achievement has been miraculous. Bookmakers, vulgar vice-presidents and duchesses have been persuaded to travel together in the expensive first-class cabin, and an extraordinary range of passengers, of all conceivable tastes, ages, incomes and backgrounds, has been fed, amused, and made reasonably happy for hours at a time, in the tourist class.

In considering the revolution which has taken place during the past twenty-five years, the most useful point to begin is probably with the meals. Until the early 1950s, some airlines were still attempting to feed as many of their passengers as possible on the ground, but others, such as Air France, preferred to serve meals in the aircraft, in order to make flights less tedious for passengers. In 1951 it was calculated that, on an average of all long-distance services, about 60 per cent. of all meals were served on the aircraft. The cramped conditions in aircraft galleys made it essential that, as far as possible, meals should be prepared before the food was put on board so that they merely had to be kept hot or heated-up in the galley. With the equipment and processes available at that time, this presented considerable problems if the meals were still to taste reasonably fresh by the time

54 July 1946. The passenger reception tents at Heathrow Airport, London

they were eaten and if the endless repetition of cold dishes was to be avoided. The introduction of deep-frozen food in about 1950 seemed to have provided the answer to most of the caterers' difficulties. By this means a complete meal was first cooked and then put in a temperature of 30 degrees below zero Fahrenheit for three or four hours. Afterwards it could be kept in cold storage for very long periods, at a temperature of −5 degrees Fahrenheit, and taken to the aircraft as required. On board it was put into electric ovens for de-frosting and heated to the required temperature.

The results were not to everyone's liking, but, like all forms of standardisation, they offered a reliable, if unexciting, product anywhere in the world at any time of the year. If hot meals were to be provided at all hours and in all climates, this was one way to do the job. The phrase 'airline meal' has subsequently become almost synonymous with predictable food that can be eaten reasonably easily with the elbows kept tightly against the body; but, given the circumstances, the only real alternative was sandwiches, and in hot climates sandwiches have a way of not remaining agreeable for very long after they are cut – and, in 1950, polythene wrappings were still experimental.

The advantages of deep-frozen food were quickly realised – the elimination of waste and unnecessary weight, the small space in which the frozen meals can be packed, and the ease of preparing them aboard the aircraft. But, in fact, the idea did not catch on as quickly as might have been expected. Little came of plans to establish refrigerated stores of deep-frozen food at stops along the route where local catering facilities had proved unsatisfactory and in 1952 BOAC, for example, was using deep-frozen food only on services starting from London, and even then for no more than a quarter of all meals. The main drawback was the weight of equipment required to prepare the food from the frozen state, but personal and national prejudices also played a part. American passengers appeared to have no objection to it, but for many years Air France refused to use frozen food at all. Their catering adviser agreed that it tasted perfectly good, but added the crushing comment, 'Mon Dieu! Who wants to eat food cooked two years ago?', and continued with his *Terrine de Caneton Nantaise* and *Cœur de Charollais sauté aux champignons*, prepared in the airport kitchens and put on board the airliner in portable refrigerated containers.

Subsequent developments have included the use of large thermos containers, which retain the original heat for up to six hours, and of new types of equipment specially designed to save weight. These included plastic tableware, nowadays found generally acceptable, but which, in its early days, was rather thick and clumsy, obtainable only in crude colours and tasting peculiar. It was, even so, an economic necessity for the airlines to experiment continuously in this field, as in others, because the larger post-war aircraft had to be made to pay, which meant keeping costs as low as possible and thereby filling as many seats as possible.

It was worked out early in the 1950s that galley equipment and food amounted to a total weight of about twelve pounds for each passenger carried. The weight of actual food carried aboard the transatlantic Constellations was 400 pounds, which was sufficient for two main meals and light refreshments for the forty-three passengers and the crew. The bar stocks amounted to a further 104 pounds, making 504 pounds in all. This, together with the weight of the stewards, was and is an important factor in airline economics, bearing in mind that the value per annum of each pound of weight saved was reckoned to be about £20.

During the later 1940s and the 1950s a considerable amount of research was carried out in order to discover the effect of air travel on food and wine. On the whole, white wines were found to withstand vibration and differences of pressure and temperature better than red; and, of the red wines, Bordeaux do better than Burgundy, champagne fares best of all. Some foodstuffs, such as cream and mayonnaise, appeared to be adversely affected by the dry atmosphere of the pressurised cabin and were not included in menus until suitable air-tight containers were developed.

One great advantage of the pressurised cabin from the caterer's point of view was that it removed most of the restrictions once considered necessary in planning meals for passengers whose digestion might have been impaired through shortage of oxygen. The main criterion for an aircraft meal is that it must be one which is acceptable to the largest number of people. It must not include dishes which are known to have only a limited appeal. Airline meals have to be as safe as possible, since the choice is always very limited, even in first class. The wider the social range of passengers became, the less adventurous the in-flight meals could be, although, in fact, the airlines have managed to change popular habits a good deal over the years.

Pressurised cabins, which have been standard for twenty years, were not, of course, introduced mainly in order to solve caterers' problems. The aim was to make it possible to fly above the weather, at altitudes where clear skies and calm air would give both pilots and passengers a more agreeable flight, and where, incidentally, the aircraft would use a good deal less fuel. Experiments[3] to achieve this went on throughout the 1920s and 1930s and, partly as a result of research and partly of a number of disasters, the manufacturers and the airlines gradually discovered how to make pressurised aircraft both acceptable to passengers and safe. Many important lessons were learnt: for instance, that smoking increases the effects of altitude and that babies and young children tolerate high altitudes better than old people do.[4] Nowadays designers usually maintain a cabin altitude of between 5,000 and 6,000 feet when the aircraft is flying at 35,000 feet.

The pressurised cabin is not, however, an altogether unmixed blessing. Passengers making a long journey, say between London and New York, are likely to experience an unusual degree of fatigue for a considerable time afterwards. This phenomenon is now so well known that some large firms make a practice of instructing their employees to take no important decisions within a period of twenty-four hours after reaching their destination. Experienced travellers have, of course, learnt to safeguard themselves in this way without being told to do so. Flying hangovers are all too real to be ignored, although some show-business people and notably Mr David Frost, have been hurling themselves out of a transatlantic aeroplane and into a television studio once a week for several years, without, in their own opinion,

55 1970. Preparing in-flight meals at SAS central
kitchen, Copenhagen. Boxes containing special
kosher meals can be seen on the left

any ill-effects on their performance. Politicians, too, are apt to fulfil engagements
remarkably soon after completing a long flight, although neither Mr Frost nor Mr
Brezhnev, it is true, has to endure the discomfort and exhaustion of economy-class
seating in addition to the devitalising influence of a pressurised cabin.

It is not, perhaps, generally realised that on scheduled flights the feeding of passengers in economy class is very strictly controlled by the International Air Traffic Authority (IATA).[5] For meals other than breakfast, airlines are permitted to offer only the following:

> One glass of fruit juice or one cup of soup or one canapé
> Bread, biscuits, butter
> Either one entrée and two vegetables, or one entrée, one vegetable and a salad
> One piece of fruit, or one pastry or one piece of chocolate
> Cheese

The quantity of bread, biscuits and cheese is not specified, and an airline which felt inclined to curry favour with its passengers in this way could legally provide great quantities of these commodities. What would, however, cause serious repercussions would be any attempt to serve both fruit juice and soup. In practice, 'one piece of fruit' is almost unknown. It is generally interpreted to mean a small quantity of canned fruit salad, sometimes with ice cream, sometimes not.

It is only fair to note, however, that some airlines manage much better than others in serving attractive meals, while remaining strictly within the IATA rules. Some make a more satisfactory job of advertising their in-flight meals than of actually providing and serving them. The problem of eating any meal in the cramped conditions of economy class is a serious one. Unless the aircraft is providentially half-empty, the food has to be transfered from tray to mouth with elbows tight against hips, to avoid knocking against the arm of one's neighbour, and this necessarily restricts the type of food that can be offered. It has to be easy to divide into mouthfuls with a plastic knife and fork, and easy to pick up and lift in a reasonably foolproof manner. Much the safest and quickest way of going about the business, as experienced travellers know very well, is to return to one's sensible childhood habits and use a spoon.

There are no regulations as to the meals which may be offered to first-class passengers and consequently gluttony on a remarkable scale is encouraged in this section of the aircraft. At the end of 1969 a connoisseur in these matters conducted a survey of what various airlines put in front of him. 'The best meal we had', he decided, 'was Pan Am's: a choice of 17 aperitifs, a choice of two hors d'œuvres, including caviare, turtle soup and sherry; a choice of six entrées; cheese; a dessert; fresh fruit; coffee. With it, a choice of champagne, Burgundy or Bordeaux, and afterwards any one of six liqueurs.'[6]

The alcohol served to first-class passengers is free, but in economy class one must pay for everything. Passengers who may be annoyed by the time and energy which stewards and stewardesses devote to what often appears to be their first priority, selling drinks and cigarettes, should remember that on some airlines, the commission they receive for this is a not unimportant part of their income.

The airlines are forbidden to give economy-class passengers even the smallest present, but for first class, once again, the situation is different. In 1969 TWA, for instance, gave a toilet kit in a zipper bag. The contents included a face cloth, toothbrush and toothpaste, comb, astringent pads, emery board, orange sticks, shoe-cleaning pad, hand lotion and after-shave lotion.

One feature of all this is usually kept as quiet as possible. First class does not pay, despite the much higher fares, and it is, in fact, subsidised by economy class, an interesting example of the poor paying for the rich.

Passengers with experience of flying before 1939 have nearly always commented on the extremely tight seating-pattern of post-war aircraft. It should be realised in this connexion that the airlines were, and still are, given no choice in the matter. They have agreed, as members of IATA, not to give economy-class passengers – the great majority – more than a certain amount of room. The reasons for this curious and, by passengers, much-resented decision are somewhat complicated. If we assume an aircraft in which the whole of the passenger cabin is devoted to first-class seating, with the appropriate standard of density and comfort, the total

56 The competitor: coaches on French Railways' 'Mistral', 1971

revenue for each flight would be £*x* or $*x*, reckoning that every seat was filled. If, however, only one quarter of the cabin is to contain first-class seats and three-quarters economy class, then the three-quarters of economy class must yield as much revenue as the same space could have done if it had been first-class. With the great difference in seat prices, these results can clearly be achieved only by putting the economy-class seats much closer together. The resulting discomfort, it was hoped, might persuade at least some passengers to travel first class, a form of motivation which the airlines continue to use.

A recent BOAC advertisement, for instance, reads:

If you want a man to do a first-class job, give him a first-class ticket.

Economy class travel looks like sound company policy. On paper.

In practice, just how sound is it?

Think of what you're asking your man to do.

Make decisions that could affect the future of your company. Decisions that rely on clear thinking.

He'll need to be as rested and relaxed as possible. Ready to go into action as soon as he reaches his destination.

And that's how first class will get him there.

More relaxed, because he's travelling in greater space and comfort. More rested, because there are fewer people and fewer disturbances.

And, psychologically, that first class ticket does a lot for his image and yours. It tells him you think he's the best man for the job.

So give him a first class ticket. And he'll do the first class job.

➤ BOAC
takes good care of you.

The exact details were laid down in 1957, in the first instance for the North Atlantic service, where the competition was fiercest and the potential greatest. What was prescribed, in order to prevent one airline treating passengers better than another, was

A maximum seat pitch (the distance from the front edge of one seat to front edge of the seat immediately in front when both are in an upright position) of 34 inches shall not be exceeded except for technical or safety reasons.

The distance between the front edge of seats (measured in an upright position) facing a bulkhead and the bulkhead shall not exceed 20 inches.

The maximum possible number of seats abreast shall be fitted as calculated by taking a normal aisle and assuming the following seat widths, measured from edge to edge outside armrests:

    1. single seat = 23 inches
    2. double seat = 42 inches
    3. triple seat = 61 inches[7]

The maximum pitch in first class is 42 inches, whereas in economy class it is 34 inches, but experienced passengers will be aware that neither are generous dimensions, and that five or six hours spent in one of these seats is a far from comfortable business. It is true that it is better to be cramped for five to six hours than for ten or twelve and that the steadily increasing speeds of aircraft have fortunately brought about a corresponding reduction in the length of the passenger's subjection. In this sense, the congestion of tourist or economy class (in the early days it was known, in a more genteel fashion, as 'coach class') probably matters less now than it did twenty years ago. There is, nevertheless, a certain mystery about economy-class seating. Few people travel with a tape measure in order to check up on such matters, but all seasoned travellers, especially those who, like the present author, have long legs, know perfectly well that the seats on some aircraft and on some airlines do somehow give that extra inch of knee-room which makes all the difference between hell and a tolerable journey. And many people must have discovered that, on certain types of aircraft, the rows running between the emergency exits provide space almost equal to first class.

The new-style air travel introduced after the war has certainly produced its critics. One of them was Mr Robert L. Turner, General Traffic Manager of Eastern Airlines. In 1950 he attended a meeting of the Society of Automotive Engineers in New York, where he read a paper called 'Air Speed Doesn't Mean a Thing'. In this paper[8] he outlined some of the shortcomings of the modern aircraft from the traffic manager's, and incidentally the passenger's, point of view. 'Some of us in the sales end of the airline business', he told his audience, 'have often felt that transport airplanes were designed by, first, making the pilot comfortable;

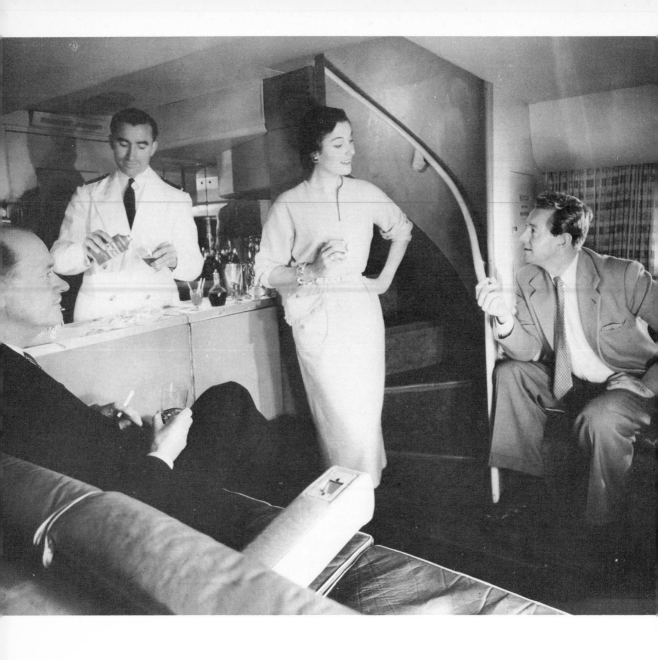

57 BOAC Stratocruiser. 1950. First-class cocktail lounge on lower deck

secondly, making it easy to maintain; thirdly, providing enough gas capacity for the range desired, and last, taking what is left over and saying this is where and how we will move the traffic.'

Mr Turner went on to list a number of the items which customers said they would like to see in an aircraft. The first was better visibility.

They want to be able to see out. With the advent of aircraft operating at high altitudes with pressurized cabins, you may think this becomes less important. However, immediately after take-off and while approaching for a landing, the customers want to see the country. In addition, one of the features of air travel which the customers like to see is cloud effects at high altitudes, particularly at sunrise and sunset – so let's fix it so the customer, even on the aisle seats, can see outside the aircraft. Some improvement can be made over certain modern airplanes, even without enlarging the windows, by relating the position of the windows to the position of the seats. Another thing: what can you do for the majority of customers who sit directly over the wing of all modern transports? The only thing they can see is some beautiful shiny aluminium.

Second was less noise:

We need to provide a quieter ride for passengers. Unquestionably there has been a lot of improvement in recent years but we have a long way to go. In my opinion, only a small part of the present day problem is engine and propeller noise. In some modern aircraft, the noise from the ventilating system is a source of annoyance to passengers. I have been in certain aircraft where the noise of air flowing through the outlets has made ordinary conversation completely impractical.

Meals should be served more quickly:

We must have the ability to serve meals quickly but in a way that will create the impression of gracious, unhurried service. We are already at the point where it takes three hundred miles to serve a meal in the modern transport. Some provision must be made to serve a palatable meal rapidly. This is another reason why it is important that the aircraft for local operations have the ability to get to smooth air quickly – no one likes to wear their meal.

Baggage handling must be faster and more convenient:

Today we fly between Washington and New York in one hour block to block. Does it make any sense for the customer to wait up to 25 minutes in order to get his baggage at the other end? This is what is sometimes happening today. Even in recent years, new aircraft have come out with completely inadequate cargo space. Please give us room to stow the stuff and make it easy for us to get to it.

Also, we need to provide more facilities for carrying baggage in the cabin. Every day we get more and more commuters – the kind of business that really pays off because we get the revenue with a minimum of sales expense. These people want to carry their baggage with them and to get going as soon as they hit the ground. Why do we put overhead racks in an airplane and then turn round and tell the customers they can't use them for anything heavier than a hat or overcoat?

The disadvantages mentioned by Mr Turner were, of course, shared equally by first- and economy-class passengers. It is interesting to notice that he put in no plea for more room for each passenger. This was evidently considered to be an unrealistic thought, a commercial impossibility. Nor was anything said about increased safety. Safety, though, is difficult to measure. The aim must be to have no accidents at all. This is probably impossible to achieve, although in 1970 there was no fatality on US domestic routes, a figure which most passengers would consider very good. For countries belonging to the International Civil Aviation Association, a total of 957 passengers were killed in 1969, 700 in 1970 and 820 in 1971.[9] In the five years between 1965 and 1970 Japan Air Lines were the safest in the world, closely followed by Swissair. The differences between individual airlines are not very great, however. For the period 1962–66, both BEA and BOAC had 0.5 accidents per 100,000 flights, Air France 0.3 and Qantas 0.55. On scheduled services, the fatality figures were[10]

	Passengers killed per 100 million passenger miles
United Kingdom	0.76
United States	0.25
Australia	0.14
France	0.85

It has been reckoned[11] that during recent years 50 per cent. of the accidents to civil aircraft have occurred in the landing phase, 30 per cent. en route, mostly in the form of crashes into rising terrain, and 20 per cent. on take-off.

It is an odd fact of aviation history that, although today's airlines and airports are provided with electronic control, navigational and landing equipment of a complexity which would have seemed almost a fairy-tale before the outbreak of war in 1939, fog brings an airport to a standstill as surely in 1971 as it did thirty or forty years ago. Without radar and an effective, reliable communication system between air and ground, both war-time developments, the task of the modern air-traffic controller, often dealing with one aircraft movement every minute, would be impossible, and without modern navigational aids flying and landing in bad weather and at night would be extremely hazardous. Yet, despite advancing technology, flights are no more punctual now than they were twenty years ago, most of the delays being due to fog, snow, ice and other weather hazards and to sheer congestion at the airports.

Faced with congested airports and tedious and uncomfortable journeys and with the high fares the airlines say are essential if they are to avoid bankruptcy, passengers have discovered a number of ways of defending themselves. One method considerably used by people who fly a great deal, is to join a travellers' club designed specially for them. Pan Am, for example, has its Clipper Clubs at many of the larger airports. At Heathrow, London, members – who always travel first class – get free drinks in a private waiting room, decorated and furnished in a New England style. This allows them to avoid the bustle of the ordinary departure lounges, and, instead of a loudspeaker summons to proceed to a boarding gate, they receive a discreet telephone call to tell them that their plane is waiting. BOAC objects to these clubs, but BEA has its Executive Clubs, with suites at Heathrow and Manchester. The privileges of belonging to an Executive Club include reserved

58 Airline advertising: the non-technical approach, 1971

131

59 Interior of one of the tents used at Heathrow during the immediate post-war period

60 Terminal 1, Heathrow, London, 1971. Passenger check-in points

car-parking at Heathrow, a guarantee that one will be protected against the misfortune of missing a flight announcement and, perhaps most valued of all, a good chance of securing a seat when the plane is officially fully booked.

The most popular way of breaking the airlines' price ring is to travel on a charter flight. The classic, but now obsolescent, definition laid down that a charter flight was restricted to a group which had principal aims and objectives other than travel and sufficient affinity, before application for a charter flight, to distinguish it from the general public. To qualify, prospective passengers must have been members of such a group for at least six months before the date of the outward flight.

It is well known, however, that the conditions can be made flexible, if not avoided altogether. A very successful British organisation, the Seven Seas Fellowship, solves the problem in an ingenious and entirely legal fashion, by declaring itself to be a body which exists 'to help those with family, friends and relatives overseas, and to assist them to overcome the problems of separation'. It employs area secretaries, who run not very demanding social and sports programmes and who are obliged to hold, or at least to call, two meetings a year. The annual subscription is £2·50 and Seven Seas prides itself on its ability to get people to any point in the world for less than half the scheduled fare.

The Seven Seas Fellowship is concerned mainly, if not entirely, with transport and with making a profit from the activity. Those firms which provide packaged holidays and tours are in a different situation. They are free to bargain with hotels and aircraft companies on whatever terms they can achieve, with the result that it is possible to fly from Manchester to Majorca and to spend two weeks there, with all one's food and accommodation covered, for considerably less than the normal fare on a scheduled flight. Eventually, the combined pressure of the tour and charter operators and of the economic necessity to fill more seats will probably force the airlines to make substantial reductions in the price of scheduled flights.

The present (1971) arguments over the ways of introducing cheaper transatlantic fares are a pointer to the future. Broadly speaking, the difference of opinion has been between those airlines which are prepared to offer seats at much less than the standard rate – about two-thirds – to passengers who are willing to make reservations, and pay, at least three months in advance; and the German airline, Lufthansa, which wants a reduction without any strings attached to it. The theory is that people travelling on business would continue to pay the full fare, while tourists, students and other impoverished travellers would choose the book-ahead, Early Bird scheme. Preliminary research, based on bookings for the first few months of 1972, has revealed a rather different and, to the airlines, disappointing pattern, since expense-account men have shown themselves to be enthusiasts for Early Bird, while the total volume of business has shown little sign of increasing at all.

61 1971. Jet Secretaries on British United Airways
England–East Africa service. Their office is in
the forward section of the VC-10

If the number of transatlantic passengers is going to rise in 1972, the evidence
available at the moment suggest that it is the charter companies, not the airlines,
who are going to benefit. Apart from the Icelandic company it is certainly not
the airlines, at least on regular services, who are likely to be transporting the very
large numbers of students who move in both directions across the Atlantic during
the summer months.

There is a further point to be considered in connexion with these pay-now-travel-
three-months-later flights. The customer is, in effect, lending the airline quite a
substantial sum of money for three months, free of interest. Many concerns, not
in the airline world, would consider this is a very desirable way of financing their
business. And the passenger has, of course, to add to the price of his ticket the

62 Half a century of technical progress

interest which he could have got on his own money if it had been invested on his behalf for the same period.

One sad, but probably inevitable, consequence of the increased size and speed of aircraft was the decline in the quality of the hostesses. To begin with, as we have already noted, all the airlines employed only registered nurses for this job, although even before the war this rule was relaxed and any girls with a good general education were eligible. For a few years after the end of the war in 1945, to be an air hostess was to be in a glamorous and much sought-after occupation, with a considerably above-average chance of making a financially excellent marriage. Many girls were undoubtedly attracted more by this kind of fringe benefit than by the salary, which was not high, or by the opportunity for foreign travel, although foreign travel and the fringe benefit might well be closely connected in some cases. By the early 1950s, however, the job was becoming much less attractive. The crowded cabins were more difficult to work in and the speed and size of the aircraft made it necessary to serve a good many meals in a very short time. The hostesses were soon spending two-thirds of their time as flying waitresses or barmaids, and although trips abroad had some attractions, it was no longer possible to find the same standard of recruit, although efficient training methods have been known to work wonders with not very promising material. Yet, despite the arduous and rather mundane conditions of work today, there appears to be no shortage of girls anxious to become air hostesses. The qualifications of most of them, unfortunately, fall far short of the minimum standard.

If it is true, at least in certain respects, that passengers in the 'sixties and 'seventies have been receiving worse treatment than passengers in the 'thirties, what do today's passengers think about the service they get? What, in fact, has been the effect of the switch from the pre-war 'everybody-is-a-VIP' treatment to the post-war 'a-passenger-is-just-a-transport-unit' approach? All the airlines have passenger relations departments, which carry out continuous research into the success of current policies, but, understandably, they are very unwilling to make public the results of this research. One company which has very kindly made such information available to us is Loftleidir, which specialises in flying passengers between Luxemburg and New York, via Iceland.

Loftleidir, because of its peculiar route, is able to avoid the North Atlantic fare agreement and in this way to undercut the major airlines. Its aeroplanes are consequently well filled, mainly by people who are not at all well-to-do. Of the several hundred different occupations given by the 6,000 passengers who completed a questionnaire in 1970, those most commonly represented were:

Students	1,875
School teachers	458
Housewives	393
University teachers	216
Secretaries	171
Engineers	159
Nurses	102

Among the questions that were asked, three have a direct bearing on what has been discussed earlier in this chapter.

Quality of meal
25·6 per cent. find it excellent; 49·9 per cent. good; 20·2 per cent. fair, and 4·3 per cent. poor.

Stewardess attitude
46·8 per cent. excellent; 43·0 per cent. good; 8·9 per cent. fair and 1·3 per cent. poor.

Comfort of seats
16·8 per cent. excellent; 47·5 per cent. good; 27·6 per cent. fair and 3·7 per cent. poor.

If Loftleidir's passengers can be considered reasonably typical of the travelling public which goes by air, the airlines would seem to have little to complain about. Mass-transport appears to produce reasonably satisfied customers. Twenty-five years of skilled publicity has had its reward.

But there are always the inconvenient survivors from better days, the veterans with nostalgic memories. Mrs Leonie Smith made frequent flights to European cities before 1939. After the war, she much preferred to go by train. 'Having flown in comfort, with VIP treatment of every passenger,' she said,[12] 'I couldn't bear to be herded like cattle.' She admitted, too, to suffering from claustrophobia under today's flying conditions, with so many people crowded into such a small space.

It is, of course, true that what one has never had, one is hardly likely to miss. Mrs Smith was unfortunate, perhaps, in having known better days, when each passenger was treated by the airlines as an important individual and the steward held a lady's hand as she walked down the steps from the aeroplane. Very few of the people who fly now have any personal experience of flying in the grand days. In the 1970s a trip by air is something to be accomplished as quickly as possible. Passengers accept it as normal that they will travel jammed tightly up against one another, with just about enough room to keep their elbows out of their neighbour's meal-tray. What few of them realise, however, is that today's first class is itself a poor substitute for the conditions made available to all passengers on the international routes before the war. The airlines have a very selective attitude to history. There are some things they prefer to allow to slip out of the memory. One may be permitted to doubt Pan American's claim, made in an advertisement issued in Britain at the beginning of 1970, that the Boeing 747 is 'the most comfortable plane ever to take the air'.

Comfort is, however, very difficult to define. Comfortable for people of what size, we might reasonably ask, of what age and with what previous experience of travel? What is one's yardstick of comfort? There must be few travellers who could honestly say that the chairs provided for them in an airliner are as comfortable as those they left behind at home or as those they find in a modern train or large motor car. There is, in fact, much less leg-room and bottom-room in an airliner than in the front of a British Leyland Mini. The airlines cater for a standard-sized passenger, of very modest dimensions. Anyone bigger is likely to remember the luxury of a first-class railway compartment with considerable nostalgia. One important difference between the first-class or, for that matter, the second-class railway coach and the modern airliner is that, until very recently and then only under great pressure, the airlines have made no attempt to provide non-smoking accommodation for their passengers. Towards the end of 1971, BOAC – a pioneer in this respect – decided to reserve one area, or compartment, of their Boeing 747s

63 The non-athletic have problems. Disembarking
from a Junkers F.13, c. 1930

for non-smokers and to request, but not compel, smokers to occupy seats in a
particular part of their 707s and VC-10s. Many of the other airlines have now begun
to follow the BOAC example and even, more curiously, to have a few non-smoking
rows at the back of their single-cabin aeroplanes.

Each new technical advance in flying needs to be examined very carefully from
the passengers' point of view, to see if the much publicised advantages are cancelled
out by disadvantages which did not previously exist. An excellent example of this
is provided by supersonic aircraft. The amount of damage to buildings which
these aircraft are likely to cause will only be demonstrated when they are in regular
service, although there is evidence enough already from test flights that it will be
both substantial and cumulative. Old buildings in particular may be seriously
weakened by repeated pressure waves from planes flying at supersonic speeds.

64 Airports must go farther out. The increasing impossibility
of urban locations. Newark Airport, New Jersey

65 (*opposite*) Too close to buildings. Lambert Field, St Louis

Socially, the advantages of such aircraft may turn out to be very dubious indeed. An important factor to consider is the certainty that supersonic planes, like Concorde and its successors, will need very long runways. To make these possible, and at the same time to minimise the chances of the sonic boom occurring over land, the airports will need to be built in fairly remote places and therefore at a considerable distance from major cities, so that passengers will have to accustom themselves either to absurdly long and expensive journeys to reach the airport or quite possibly to a change of plane, with a slower aircraft or a helicopter undertaking the first stretch of the journey. Under such circumstances, the city centre to city centre time for a journey between say, Frankfurt and New York may be little less than it is at present, using much slower aircraft. In some places, large investment may be undertaken in order to provide monorail or other rapid railway connexion between the town terminal and the airport, so that the speed advantages of the supersonic planes may not be completely lost. By that time, too, one must surely expect that airports

66 Anchorage, Alaska, 1970. The third busiest air-centre. Alaskans travel more miles per person than any other people in the world

67 The airport – town–terminal bottleneck, as seen by *Punch* in 1939

will have been made much more independent of weather conditions than they are at the moment. Operators, and passengers, will not be able to tolerate a situation in which an enormously expensive supersonic aircraft, scheduled to make three round-trips a day between London and New York, is immobilised for many hours because of fog. Delays of this kind are sufficiently serious and frustrating with conventional aircraft. With the coming of supersonic planes they will be economically and politically disastrous. Concorde passengers are not likely to be patient.

It is curious that, although the promoters of the Concorde supersonic airliner have made great play of the fact that Concorde will convey passengers from London to New York in two hours, instead of the present tedious seven, they find no problem in assuring people that they are going to enjoy the twelve-hour Concorde journey to Australia. A flight of only one to two hours is really no more than a bus-ride, but, for reasons of prestige, the impresarios of Concorde would not like the public to feel that they were providing a bus-service across the Atlantic. That function, ironically, is reserved for the much slower Boeing 747s.

Those with personal knowledge of existing air-bus services expect reliability and convenience, not comfort or personal attention. The shuttle services, such as that covering the New York–Washington route, which are operated in a number of densely populated areas of the United States, are strictly utilitarian affairs. Many people now use them as normal methods of commuting between their work and their home. There is no prior booking. A stewardess issues tickets on the plane, mostly against credit-cards – cash is not greatly liked – and, if one plane is full, there is another standing by to take the overflow. A similar system is obviously required for such busy, short-distance routes as London–Paris, London–Brussels and London–Amsterdam and it will certainly come during the next five years, with the airlines emphasising 'efficiency' and 'convenience', but certainly not 'comfort'. Two hundred or three hundred miles, by today's standards, is too short a distance for comfort.

As flying becomes more 'normal' each year, there is some disagreement as to whether it is safer or more dangerous than it used to be. The congestion above major airports has certainly put an appalling degree of responsibility on both pilots and controllers, and it is probably better that passengers should not be aware of the number of near-misses which occur daily around the world. It is also true that, with large, pressurised aircraft, an accident, when it occurs, is very likely to be a bad one, with few, if any, survivors. The airlines show a remarkable degree of optimism in the face of this situation. Only one of them gives passengers the extra safety of rear-facing seats, the exception being the Royal Air Force, which operates the safest airline in the world. None of them, the RAF included, pads the backs of the seats. The passengers may have the emergency oxygen apparatus demonstrated to them, but they are never told that unless they get it clapped against their faces in a matter of seconds, a feat rather difficult for an old person or a mother with two small children, they will be dead.

The airlines have always measured safety in terms of casualties per mile or per million miles flown. This system has been forcefully criticised by Vernon W. Lowell, a pilot employed by TWA for many years, in his book *Airline Safety is a Myth*, published in 1967. Mr Lowell challenged the per-mile calculation and said the question which ought to be asked is, 'What are your chances of being killed if you spend an hour in a plane, a car, a bus or a train?' On this basis, he discovered that air travel is 30 per cent. more dangerous than car travel, or, putting the difference the other way round, that a bus is twenty times safer than a plane and a train thirty times safer.

While on the subject of accidents, it might perhaps be mentioned that the insurance which air travellers are skilfully persuaded to take out to cover injury, death or loss of their baggage is largely unnecessary, because the airlines are legally bound to pay compensation in these matters, and, in the event, a passenger, or his executor, is extremely unlikely to be paid twice over. The sole value of the private insurance certificate is to provide evidence that the passenger said, on a given date, that his baggage was worth a stated sum and that he paid a premium on this basis. Such an assertion can, however, be a complete falsehood and a good lawyer would find no great difficulty in demolishing an unrealistic claim.

One of the favourite pastimes of the public relations departments maintained by the American airlines is to compile lists of the 'firsts', innovations pioneered by the airline in question. An examination of two of these lists shows that very few of the items they contain have much to do with the comfort of passengers, although convenience and comfort are, of course, not always easy to distinguish. What such lists do mark is the progressive achievement of a reliable means of moving large numbers of people rapidly over long distances. One item on the much-publicised Pan American list reads 'First airline to propose a plan for low cost mass transportation on a world-wide basis.'

This can be viewed, according to one's tastes and prejudices, either as an announcement of inevitable doom or as the ultimate in efficiency and progress. What is certain is that the airlines have been working to such a policy for the past twenty-five years and that the travelling public has been compelled to accept it, or to cease to travel, except on those highly-favoured routes where the alternatives of sea or rail transport are still available.

Some of the official Pan Am 'firsts', such as '1950: First commercial airline to enter the Korean airlift', are not likely to appear of great significance to historians. Others, however, are reflections of the real technical advances pioneered by this

68 What the passenger doesn't see. The Boeing 747 control cabin (*see key overleaf*)

BOEING 747 CONTROL CABIN

Although considerably larger, the control cabin of a 747 is less complex than that of a 707. The major portion of the instrumentation in a 747 control cabin is identified in this picture of a Trans World Airlines superjet cockpit:

1--Overhead switch panel
2--Standby compass
3--Navigational radio selector
4--Autopilot engage switch
5--Navigation mode selector
6--Speed mode selector
7--Airplane registry no.
8--Map, panel light knobs
9--Central instrument warning lights
10--Approach progress indicators
11--Inertial navigation warning lights
12--Thrust reverser indicator lights
13--Pitch trim controls
14--Clock
15--Mach/airspeed indicator
16--Gyro horizon
17--Electric altimeter
18--Radio altimeter
19--Navigation marker beacon lights
20--Total air temperature
21--Gear down/locked indicators
22--Microphone switch
23--Autopilot disengage
24--Nose gear tiller
25--Chart holder
26--Pilot's control yoke
27--Horizontal direction indicator
28--Vertical speed indicator
29--Standby altimeter
30--Engine pressure ratio gauges
31--Lowspeed engine comp.
32--Exhaust gas temp.
33--High speed engine compressor RPM
34--Fuel flow indicator
35--Flap position indicator
36--Static air temp.
37--Turn and bank indicator
38--Flight control position indicator
39--Annunciator light panel
40--True airspeed indicator
41--Landing gear control handle
42--Radio magnetic indicator
43--Instrument switches
44--Reserve brakes
45--Speed brake handle
46--Thrust levers
47--Inertial navigation controls
48--Brake pressure
49--Water injection control
50--Computer selector switch
51--Weather radar sco
52--Rudder pedal
53--Manual stabilizer trim levers
54--Go-around switche
55--Flap lever
56--Pitch trim
57--Parking brake lat
58--Parking brake lig
59--Engine start leve
60--Stabilizer trim cutout switche
61--Seat arm, down position
62--Weather radar cor panel
63--Automatic directi finder
64--Air traffic contr transponder
65--Very high frequen radio
66--Ultra high freque radio
67--Aileron trim
68--Rudder trim
69--Warning horn silencer
70--Seat positioning controls
71--Pilot's handset for intercom and passenger announ
72--Seat arm, up posi

69 Controlling the Boeing 747

enterprising airline. It was, for instance, the first, in 1937, to operate in continuous service a transport aircraft with pressurised cabin. TWA, after being the first U.S. carrier to go all-jet across the Atlantic (1961) and the first to show 'modern in-flight motion pictures' (also 1961), achieved true fame in 1970, as the first to introduce the Boeing 747 on domestic routes in the United States.

On 19 March 1970, with the arrival of its first Boeing 747 flight from Europe, TWA dedicated Flight Wing One, the superjet-age expansion to the Trans World Flight Center at Kennedy Airport. 'First air terminal built from the ground up for the B-747, the facility is the only private airline terminal featuring Customs and other Federal Inspection Services for passengers arriving from abroad.'

The Trans World Flight Center at New York, mentioned so proudly as a miracle of commonsense and convenience, is perhaps one of the most terrifyingly efficient buildings so far designed for the processing of human beings. With its long, bare corridors, its queueing corrals and its batteries of check-through points, where passengers are scrutinised by rows of immigration officials, with faces all cast in the same dead, expressionless mould, this chromium-and-plastic cattle-market is the perfect symbol of mass, impersonal travel. This, one might feel, is the logical, inevitable conclusion of post-war policy. An enlarged version of the Boeing 747 Jumbo Jet, with a capacity of 1000 passengers, double the present number, is now in the planning stage. If and when all these seats are filled, the new monster will certainly justify the Trans World Flight Center, but whether each passenger will feel any more of an individual human being as a result seems open to doubt.

It is possible, however, to take impersonality one stage further and it is the Germans, not the Americans, who have pointed the way to final efficiency. In 1970 Friedrich Krupp, of Essen, announced its plans for a new passenger-handling technique, known as the PUT system. It is designed in the first place for the cargo versions of the Lockheed C-5 A Galaxy and the Boeing 747.

At the terminal the containers first function as mobile waiting rooms. Once the passengers have taken their seats, these containers are pushed through the opened nose gate into the fuselage of the plane. The passenger container is independent of the fuselage and furnished with everything normally found in an aircraft cabin. For each Jumbo there will be several of such passenger containers equipped with seats, luggage racks, galleys and lavatories. For lighting, air-conditioning and communications, the containers can be connected to the power supply of the terminal building or of the plane. The plane's fuselage acts as a pressurised shell.

The plane and the terminal building are linked by an overhead structure, a gantry which carries a lifting platform fitted with rollers adapted to the floor contour of the plane. The gantry moves at right angles to the plane's centreline and the lifting platform parallel to the centreline. The platform supports the passenger

container as it is being pushed into the aircraft. The terminal building has a decentralised layout, which means that all the facilities within the area where a plane is being loaded or unloaded serve only this area. This simplifies checking-in and clearance and makes it easier for the passengers to find their way about. Access routes for bus and rail services to the airport could be run underground to keep the area in front of the building free for road traffic. For longer distances, a moving walkway would be provided to connect the car park or the helicopter landing area with the terminal buildings.

On the side facing the airfield, the terminal building of the PUT system is split at each floor level into four adjacent boxes with five roller tables capable of carrying two or three passenger containers. On each floor there will be a fourth box to accommodate stand-by containers and to serve as a repair and servicing area. After the departure of a plane the empty containers will be cleaned in the boxes.

The passenger containers will always be kept in a position where the end accommodating the sanitary equipment faces the terminal building, so that such equipment can be removed from the container for cleaning, servicing and repair, and replaced quickly by other units ready for use. This offers the advantage that servicing need no longer be done under pressure of time between landing and take-off. Out of seventeen ground service vehicles normally required for servicing a Jumbo jet, six will no longer be necessary.

A computer-controlled system will reduce checking-in time per passenger and

70, 71 Passengers in bulk. The Krupp unit transport system, 1970

luggage to thirty seconds. This figure is calculated on the basis of 120 passengers per container, a checking-in period of fifteen minutes per container and four checking-in points per box. Having checked in, passengers will enter the container, stow their luggage and take their seats. Since checking-in takes place before the plane lands, the passenger containers assume the function of the waiting rooms used today.

After landing, the plane will taxi from the airfield and will then be towed nose-inwards to the standage area. Here the nose gate will be opened, the lifting gantry moved into position and the first passenger container moved out on to the platform. Platform and gantry then move either to the lower or upper floor of the terminal building and push a passenger container into the first box. This sequence is repeated twice for the remaining two containers in the plane and three times for the three containers with waiting passengers in the boxes.

As soon as the nose gate is open, fuelling and inspections will begin. At a travelling speed of 0·5 metres per second and a mean travel distance of 35 metres per container, only about seven minutes will be required to change the passenger containers. If a multi-point hydrant system is used for fuelling, the Jumbo jet will be able to taxi back to the airfield for take-off after only ten minutes.

The Krupp research team foresees further uses for this system. In one variant the passengers would be transferred directly from airliner to waiting elevated trains for direct transportation into cities. In another variant, smaller passenger containers would be shifted from large continental airliners to smaller planes or to helicopters. According to estimates by Krupp, 500 passengers and their luggage could be exchanged in ten minutes through the use of the container system.

Since large airports such as Frankfurt's Rhine-Main are expected by 1975 to be handling 6,000 departing and arriving passengers in periods from thirty to forty-five minutes, the Krupp researchers believe that their system, or something like it, will soon be essential equipment.

This is, of course, still a few years in the future. When it comes, it will undoubtedly be hailed as a new marvel of the technological age and passengers will, once again, be told how lucky they are. The Krupp container will certainly offer the airline operator the great advantage of elasticity, since, by using this system, a large aeroplane could be filled with, say, two containers of people and two of freight, or three of people and one of freight, according to the traffic available on any particular day. The only essential difference between the two kinds of goods would be that the passengers would walk into their containers and the freight would need the help of fork-lift trucks.

REFERENCES

1

1 *Illustrated London News* 6 September 1919
2 i.e. by sea
3 A. J. Jackson *De Havilland Aircraft* 1962, p. 45
4 Recalled in *Illustrated London News* 6 September 1919
5 A. J. Jackson *British Civil Aircraft 1919–59* vol. I, p. 70, estimates that there were fifty of these enterprises in 1919–21. He lists the most successful
6 ibid.
7 This, and later quotations and references, are, unless otherwise stated, from a conversation with the author, 18 May 1970
8 Captain H. Shaw, 'The First London–Paris Service', *The Aeroplane* 14 July 1944
9 *The Aeroplane* 18 August 1944
10 See, for instance, Anne Robertson Coupar *The Smirnoff Story* 1960, pp. 60–1
11 For the beginnings and development of this type of insurance see *A Short History of Aviation Insurance in the United Kingdom* 2nd ed., 1968. This is Report H.R. 10 of the Historic Records Working Party of the Insurance Institute of London
12 Captain H. Shaw, 'Pioneering without Politics', *The Aeroplane* 18 August 1944
13 Conversation with the author, 15 June 1970
14 This was a constant hazard. In 1922, Mrs M. Fitzrandolph, a member of the Friends' Relief Service, flew from Warsaw to Prague. With storms ahead, the pilot decided to land at Breslau to take on more fuel. He told his passengers not to get out of the plane, because they had no papers, and not to talk while the plane was on the ground
15 Nowadays the Air Navigation (General) Regulations permit that, provided an aircraft has seats for twelve or more people, the passengers and crew need not be weighed. The following standard weights are assumed:

Males over 12 years	165 pounds
Females over 12 years	143 pounds
Children 2–12 years	85 pounds
Babies under 2 years	17 pounds

16 Captain H. Shaw, 'Pioneering without Politics', *The Aeroplane* 18 August 1944
17 The Air Council's agreement, setting up Imperial Airways, was with a 'Heavier-Than-Air-Transport Company to be called Imperial Air Transport Company'. It was required to use only British-made aircraft and engines, and provided it flew a specified number of miles each year it was to get an initial subsidy of £1 million

and a further £1 million over a period of ten years. Imperial Airways lasted until August 1939, when Royal Assent was given to the establishment of British Overseas Airways Corporation, which amalgamated Imperial and the smaller, privately owned, British Airways.

18 Le voyageur est encore ce qui importe le plus dans le voyage, a écrit quelque part Suares. Les Transports Aériens, en cinq années d'un prodigieux essor, ont eu le souci d'assurer à leurs passagers la sécurité et, avec le confort et l'élégance des amenagements interieurs, le bénéfice inchiffrable de la vitesse, le gain d'un temps si précieux dans la vie présente . . .

. . . Le règne de l'avion donnera au voyage sa plénitude. Le voyageur étant l'esclave de la voie ferrée, et s'il lui arrivait de s'affranchir de ce joug, l'automobile ou le bateau ne lui offraient que des horizons limités. La navigation aérienne lui ouvre 'les vastes solitudes des espaces infinies'.

L'avion permet de voir sans monotonie et sans servitude. La terre pour lui, se déroule entière et inattendue, avec la clarté de ses eaux, le calme de ses forêts, la patience de ses routes, le volonté de ses villages et de ses champs.

Au Bourget. Présentez-vous à votre pilote. Celui-ci, qui est toujours un homme du monde et un as de la guerre, vous serrera la main et résumera pour vous les prévisions du voyage . . .

19 Mrs Mary Hayman: conversation with the author, 15 June 1970
20 *Aeronautical Review* December 1924
21 *Aviation* November 1935

2

1 Founded in 1917 by a shipping and industrial combine, with the announcement that passenger and mail transport services would be organised immediately after the war
2 At Schwerin, where Fokker had established a war-time factory for supplying the German air force
3 *Ikarus* No. 1, 1925
4 *Die Luftreise* No. 1, May 1925
5 *Imperial Airways Monthly Bulletin* June 1927
6 ibid., September 1927
7 ibid.
8 ibid., March 1932
9 ibid., July 1927
10 ibid., April 1928
11 ibid., August 1927
12 ibid.
13 ibid., October 1927
14 *Guide de l'Aéroport du Bourget* 1926
15 *Imperial Airways Monthly Bulletin* January 1928
16 Communication to the author, 25 October 1970
17 *Deutsche Lufthansa: Betriebsmitteilungen* No. 7, 31 July 1928
18 *New York Times* 15 May 1970

19 Mr Walter Wren: conversation with the author, 16 June 1970
20 Hudson Fysh *Qantas Rising* 1964, p. 257
21 *Journey from Washington to Los Angeles, August 1929*, by Joseph S. Edgerton
22 Quoted in S. A. Stimpson, 'The Progress of Air Transport', *Shell Aviation News* October 1935
23 ibid.
24 *Daily Telegraph* 30 July 1971
25 *The Times* 11 July 1931
26 *Aviation* February 1932
27 Stuart Menzies *All Ways by Airways* 1932
28 Imperial Airways *Honeymoon* card, 1937
29 Imperial Airways booklet, *Special Notes to Ladies on Air Travel* 1932
30 Pistany or Piestany, Czechoslovakia, is 80 km north-east of Bratislava. It is the most important of the Slovak spas
31 Imperial Airways brochure, 1937
32 *Imperial Airways Gazette* 25 March 1938
33 En avion, une conception toute nouvelle des contrées survolées vous attend. D'un confortable fauteuil, vous aurez l'agreable surprise d'un spectacle unique et grandiose.

Plus d'accidents de terrain, d'arbres et de maisons pour vous masquer le paysage.

Une merveilleuse vue d'ensemble vous permet de saisir, simultanement et distinctement des points distants les uns des autres de plusieurs kilometres.

Ne croyez pas que la vitesse de l'avion vous empêche de jouir de ce spectacle, le paysage défile lentement et vous l'avez l'impression que l'avion est suspendu par un fil invisible alors qu'en réalité vous êtes emporté à une très grande vitesse, comme vous pouvez vous en rendre compte en passant la main par une fenêtre.

Nos lignes relient PARIS aux principaux centres européens: BRUXELLES, capitale de l'energetique Belgique; AMSTERDAM, la Venise du Nord; BERLIN, la grande centre germanique.

Ne vous imaginez pas que l'avion soit un moyen de transport ruineaux; l'essor sans cesse croissant de notre trafic nous a permis de réduire nos prix et de concurrencer maintenant ceux du chemin de fer, tout en vous offrant bien d'autres avantages.

Quelques passagères ont le mal de l'air; ne vous en effrayez pas car ce mal est bénin et intermittent et à l'inverse du mal de mer, vous pouvez d'ailleurs facilement l'éviter en utilisant le Mothersill's. Nos avions sont chauffés, néanmoins, emportez un bon manteau. Les forrures, lunettes, gants spéciaux sont inutiles.

Vous pouvez avoir toute confiance en nos pilotes, ce sont des spécialistes recrutés avec soin et d'une prudence éprouvée; d'ailleurs la plupart sont mariés et père de familles. Ne confondez pas avion sportif et avion commercial, l'un est à l'autre, ce que l'auto de course est à l'auto de tourisme – Tout est prévu pour votre securité: nous nous entourons de renseignements météorologiques qui vous permettront d'effectuer votre voyage dans les conditions les meilleures et la T.S.F. permet à nos équipages d'être continuellement, continuellement renseignés sur le temps.

Souvenez-vous des premiers voyages en chemin de fer: que de détracteurs. Les Premiers automobilistes n'étaient ils pas également considérés des déséquilibrés?

Dès 1928, grâce aux derniers perfectionnements, toute personne éclairée doit considérer l'avion comme un moyen de transport RAPIDE, ECONOMIQUE, NORMAL.

34 Imperial Airways leaflet, blue and white, with a teapot on the cover. It is interesting to see how, in aviation as in most other things, history has a way of repeating itself. In October 1971, Sunday afternoon tea-flights over London began again. The aircraft this time were Boeing 747 Jumbo Jets, chartered from BOAC by a travel agency, and the flights lasted an hour.
35 *Shell Aviation News* January 1933
36 Captain H. St G. Harpur, 'London to Dublin by Air', *Aviation*, the National Air Magazine of Ireland, August 1935
37 ibid.
38 *Shell Aviation News* December 1935

3

1 Preserved at the Musée de l'Air, Paris
2 Douglas H. Robinson *LZ 1929 'Hindenburg'* New York 1964
3 C. F. Andrews *Vickers Aircraft since 1908* 1969, pp. 31–2
4 Nevil Shute *Slide Rule* 1968, p. 103. As N. S. Norway, the author was one of the design team working on the *R.100*
5 ibid., p. 55
6 ibid., p. 55
7 ibid., p. 104
8 ibid., p. 109

4

1 *Aeronautic Review* April 1925
2 Quoted in *Aeronuatic Review* October 1926
3 He is referring to 1925–27
4 A. H. Affleck *The Wandering Years* 1964, p. 29
5 ibid., pp. 29–30
6 Later Sir Hudson Fysh, and Managing Director of the company
7 *Qantas Rising* 1965, p. 145
8 ibid., p. 162
9 ibid., p. 225
10 Communication to the author, January 1971. I am grateful to Captain Brain for much useful information about Qantas
11 16 January 1970 to Qantas. Letter communicated to the author by the company
12 *Shell Aviation News* September 1936
13 See Deruluft annual reports, in archive of Lufthansa, Cologne
14 *T.W.A. Skyliner* February 1940
15 *Aviation* June 1936

5

1 Published by Pilkington Brothers, for private circulation, in 1936, as supplements to their house magazine, *Cullet*, in April and July, under the title 'Leaves from Mr. W. H. Pilkington's Diary'

2 *Shell Aviation News* No. 18, December 1932
3 'Batavia to Amsterdam'; an article by 'Passenger' in *Shell Aviation News* August 1935. See also B. L. Falconer *Flying around the World* Boston, 1937, and H. R. Elkins *Round the World in Eighty Days* 1934
4 Conversation with the author, 1 July 1970
5 Conversation with the author, 9 June 1970
6 Sir Hudson Fysh *Qantas at War* 1968
7 Mr Walter Wren: conversation with the author, 16 June 1970
8 ibid.
9 Major E. Munday *A Report of a Flight made to London from Mpika 30th April 1932* Livingstone: Northern Rhodesia 1932
10 *Imperial Airways Gazette* September 1936
11 Mr S. C. Isaacs: conversation with the author, 9 June 1970
12 *Imperial Airways Monthly Bulletin* December 1936
13 ibid., December 1938
14 Conversation with Mr F. Zandvliet, KLM
15 *Imperial Airways Monthly Bulletin* February 1939
16 ibid., January 1939
17 *Imperial Airways Gazette* September 1937
18 *Some Aspects of the Organisation of Empire Air Services*. The second Brancker Memorial Lecture to the Institute of Transport, 23 November 1936
19 Patent No. 447,327
20 In the possession of the author.
21 *Imperial Airways Monthly Bulletin* July 1939

6

1 Published in *Aero Digest* October 1939
2 W. L. Pilkington, 'Atlantic Crossings, 1941', *Cullet* No. 53, October 1941
3 ibid.
4 The first regular aeroplane service across the South Atlantic was made by Pan American in 1939, using Boeing flying-boats. The flight took twenty-nine hours
5 The censor compelled the type of aeroplane to be omitted
6 *Cullet* Autumn 1942
7 In a conversation with the author, 2 July 1970. After the war BOAC was split into three: a new version of BOAC to fly the long-haul world routes, British South American Airways, intended to fly the South Atlantic but later re-merged with BOAC, and British European Airways

7

1 Conversation with the author, 16 June 1970
2 See Stephen Wheatcroft *Air Transport Policy* 1964, p. 14. 'The largest number of air journeys to and from this country are now being made by quite ordinary people who are making an air trip to a holiday resort or to visit friends and relatives.' Many of these passengers – 600,000 in 1962 – were carried by private airlines on inclusive

terms, and Mr Wheatcroft notes that 'a very large number of people have been converted into air travellers through the promotional efforts of the organisers of air tours'.

3 As early as 1920 the United States Air Force was making attempts to pressurise cabins, and between 1931 and 1937 Professor A. Piccard and others were succeeding with balloon flights at altitudes of up to 72,000 feet, by using pressurised gondolas

4 On such points see Dr Ross Armstrong McFarlane *Human Factors in Relation to the Development of Pressurised Cabins* 1971

5 The International Air Transport Association (IATA) was founded in 1945, as the successor to the International Air Traffic Association, which had been the regulating body for air transport since 1919. It represents the airlines of eighty countries. Its commercial objective is 'to ensure that people, cargo and mail can move anywhere on this vast global network as easily as though they were on a single airline within a single country'. In practice, this means that once a regulation or a system has been agreed, all members are bound to observe it.

6 Eric Clark, 'The Uptight World of Air Travel', *The Observer* 11 January 1970

7 TWA Memorandum *North Atlantic New Tourist Type Economy Service* 27 December 1957

8 Summarised in *Shell Aviation News* January 1951

9 *ICAO Accident Table*, published in *Flight*, January 1972. Expressed in terms of the number of miles and hours flown, the figures for fatal accidents appear to show that flying becomes safer each year.

	1969	*1970*	*1971*
Per 100 million miles flown	·77	·64	·55
Per 100,000 aircraft hours	·27	·23	·18

10 Board of Trade *The Safety Performance of U.K. Airline Operators* 1968, Appendix G, Table 3

11 A. J. Launay *Historic Air Disasters* 1967, p. 47

12 Conversation with the author, 9 June 1970

Appendix Two

1 M. D. Klaas, 'Last of the Flying Clipper Ships', *Journal of the American Aviation Historical Society* 2nd quarter, 1968

2 Peter M. Bowers *Boeing Aircraft since 1916* 1966

3 Charles H. Gibbs-Smith *Aviation* 1969, p. 200

BIBLIOGRAPHY

THE LITERATURE of aviation is very extensive. The books listed below have been selected as being easily available and of interest to the general reader, and as containing certain material which has a direct bearing on the theme of the present book – passengers and the amenities provided for them.

Excellent detailed bibliographies covering the development of aviation as a whole can be found in C. H. Gibbs-Smith, *Aviation: an Historical Survey*, and in R. E. G. Davies, *A History of the World's Airlines*.

AFFLECK, ARTHUR H. *The Wandering Years* 1964

ANDREWS, C. F. *Vickers Aircraft since 1908* 1969

BALDWIN, N. C. *Imperial Airways* 1950

BOWERS, PETER M. *Boeing Aircraft since 1916* 1966

BROOKS, P. W. *The Modern Airliner: its Origin and Development* 1961

COOPER, M. H., and MAYNARD, A. K. *The Price of Air Travel* 1971

COUPAR, ANNE ROBERTSON *The Smirnoff Story* 1960

DAVIES, R. E. G. *A History of the World's Airlines* 1964

DUVAL, G. R. *British Flying Boats and Amphibians, 1902–52* 1966

ECKNER, H. *My Zeppelins* 1958

GIBBS-SMITH, C. H. *Aviation: an Historical Survey from its Origins to the End of World War II* 1970

GIBBS-SMITH, C. H. *A History of Flying* 1953

GRUMBRIDGE, JACK L. *Marketing Management in Air Transport* 1966

HANDLEY PAGE LTD *Forty Years On* 1949

HILL, Sir RODERICK *The Baghdad Air Mail* 1929

JACKSON, A. J. *British Civil Aircraft, 1919–59* 2 vols 1959–60

LAUNAY, A. J. *Historic Air Disasters* 1967

LEHMANN, E. A. *Zeppelin* 1937

LINDBERGH, C. A. *The Spirit of St. Louis* 1953

LOCK, H. H., and CREASEY, J. *The Log of a Merchant Airman* 1941

McFARLANE, ROSS ARMSTRONG *Human Factors in Relation to the Development of Pressurised Cabins* 1971

MINISTRY OF INFORMATION *Atlantic Bridge* 1945

NIELSEN, T. *The Zeppelin Story* 1955

OLLEY, G. P. *A Million Miles in the Air* 1934
PENROSE, H. J. *British Aviation: the Pioneer Years* 1967
RUSMAN, E. *Wings Across Continents* 1935
SALT, A. E. W. *Imperial Air Routes* 1930
SHUTE, N. *Slide Rule* 1954
STROUD, J. *European Transport Aircraft since 1910* 1966
TAYLOR, J. W. R. *A Picture History of Flight* 2nd ed. 1960
TOLAND, J. *Ships of the Sky* 1957
VALTH, J. G. *Graf Zeppelin* 1959
WEYL, A. R. *Fokker: the Creative Years* 1965
WHEATCROFT, STEPHEN *Air Transport Policy* 1964
WILLIAMS, J. E. D. *The Operation of Airlines* 1964
YOUNG, M. *Civil Aviation* 1944

Some important dates
in the development of air transport

1909	First Channel crossing by aeroplane, Blériot, from Calais to Dover
1910	First air passenger service, by Zeppelin in Germany
1911	First practical seaplane flies (Curtiss)
1913	First large multi-engine aeroplane flies (Sikorsky Bolshoi in Russia)
1919	First regular and scheduled commercial airmail and passenger lines
	Inter Air Traffic Association formed
	First transatlantic flight, by stages via the Azores (U.S. NC. 4 flying-boat)
	Junkers invents aerofoil wing-flaps
	First direct non-stop transatlantic flight (Alcock and Brown, in a Vickers Vimy)
	First direct transatlantic crossing by airship (*R.34*)
	First flight from England to Australia (Ross and Smith, in a Vickers Vimy)
1920	First aeroplane with retractable undercarriage
	Tests of Zeppelin-Staaken E.4/20 four-engine all-metal passenger transport, forerunner of the modern all-metal airliner
1923	First non-stop coast-to-coast crossing of U.S.A. (Kelly and Macready)
1924	Junkers G.23 three-engine all-metal monoplane
	Imperial Airways established
1926	First flight over the North Pole (Byrd and Bennett)
1927	Lockheed Vega
1928	First flight across the Pacific, from U.S.A. to Australia (Kingsford Smith)
	Dornier DOX twelve-engine flying-boat, with 169 passengers and crew
1930	Whittle's first jet-engine patent
1931	Handley Page H.P.42 enters service with Imperial Airways
	Imperial Airways open London–Capetown service

1933   Boeing 247, the first modern-type monoplane airliner
Douglas DC-1

1934   First practical constant-speed variable pitch propellers enter airline service
Douglas DC-2 enters airline service

1935   Prototype of the Boeing 299, B.17 Flying Fortress, flies

1936   Douglas DC-3 twin-engine airliner enters service
Short Empire monoplane flying-boat first flies

1937   First fully pressurised aeroplane, Lockheed XC35
Hindenburg crashes
First modern-type four-engine aeroplane (Junkers Ju 90)

1938   First flight of Boeing 307, the first pressurised passenger-carrying aeroplane

1939   First turbojet aeroplane (Heinkel He 176)

1940   First successful flight by a single-rotor helicopter (Sikorsky VS.300)

1942   Douglas DC-4

1943   Lockheed Constellation airliner

1945   First turboprop aeroplane (Gloster Meteor)
Regular transatlantic passenger service

Aircraft which carried speed, comfort and reliability a stage further forward

Armstrong Whitworth Argosy

First delivered to Imperial Airways in 1926. A three-engined biplane, seating twenty passengers. The Captain and First Officer were put side-by-side in an open cockpit in the nose. On 1 May 1927, one of the Argosies inaugurated the world's first luxury 'named' air route, the London–Paris 'Silver Wing' lunch service. This carried a buffet and steward in place of the two rear seats.

On 15 June 1928 an Argosy raced the 'Flying Scotsman' train from London to Glasgow and won by fifteen minutes.

Avro 504 K

A wooden training aircraft, built in large numbers during the First World War. Until the De Havilland Moth was introduced in 1926, the 504 K was the most common British aeroplane. After 1918, 319 were converted for civil use by removing the dual controls and adding a third seat. They were extensively used for joy-riding.

Avro 691 Lancastrian

A civil conversion of the Lancaster bomber. BOAC used them on the Australia and New Zealand route immediately after the war, as an interim type. They flew from London to Sydney in three days and killed the pre-war system of leisurely flights with overnight stops. There was accommodation for only nine passengers and these aircraft were consequently very expensive to operate. A London–South America service was established with Lancastrians in 1946.

Boeing 247

The first transport to have wing and tail-unit de-icing. Entering service in 1934, it carried ten passengers, two pilots and a stewardess.

The 247, with the DC-1 and Lockheed Electra, was one of a group of three American aircraft which brought great changes to civil aviation. For details of this, see the note on the Lockheed Electra.

Boeing 314 Clipper

The Clipper flying-boat first flew in 1938. They maintained a regular transatlantic service between 1939 and 1945. Maximum capacity was eighty-nine passengers. 'Not even the jet-liners of today could meet the rigorous luxury standards set forth by the "Clipper". Fashionable state-rooms, and an air of opulence to the interior, which included a de-luxe suite and dining saloon.'[1] Sleeping accommodation was available, although on most services passengers slept ashore during the overnight stops.

Boeing 314 A

Three of these four-engined flying-boats were bought by the British Government in 1941, and operated on a Foynes–Lagos–Baltimore circuit until 1945. After the war they were transferred to the Baltimore–Bermuda run, carrying fifty-five passengers for £41 return.

In their six and a half years of service they flew more than four million miles, crossed the Atlantic 596 times and carried 42,000 passengers without accident or injury.

Boeing 377 Stratocruiser

The Stratocruiser was developed from the military C-97 Superfortress. Fifty-five were built in 1949–50. They had a two-deck pressurised fuselage. 'Depending on seating density and arrangement, the main passenger cabin could seat from fifty-five to one hundred passengers. When equipped as a sleeper aircraft the 377 contained twenty-eight upper and lower berth units plus five seats. A spiral staircase led to a lounge on the lower deck behind the wing that could hold an additional fourteen passengers. This was generally used as a luxury bar by the airlines and seating space in it was not sold or used to increase overall capacity. Complete dressing rooms were provided for both men and women, and the most complete galley provided to that time in a commercial airliner was installed at the rear of the cabin.'[2] Ten Stratocruisers were used by BOAC on its Montreal, New York and Caribbean services, and later to West Africa.

BOAC operated three grades of Stratocruiser flights across the Atlantic, 'Monarch' (superluxury), 'Majestic' (first class, with fifty passengers) and 'Coronet' (tourist, eighty-one passengers).

Boeing 707

This very important aircraft first flew in 1954. By the end of the 1950s it was in service with many of the world's airlines. They were planned as medium- to long-range transports, but the first 707s were flown on the Atlantic route, with a reduced payload. There have been many modifications to meet customers' particular requirements. A typical version accommodated 189 tourist passengers, cruised at 600 mph and had a range of about 6,000 miles.

The 727 had a similar performance but a shorter range.

Boeing 747 Jumbo Jet

The first production model flew in 1968. The 747 takes up to 490 passengers or 110 tons of cargo. Two separate aisles allow for seating up to ten abreast. This huge plane operates with a flight crew of three and a cabin staff of about thirty.

Douglas DC-2 and DC-3

This very popular twin-engined aeroplane appeared in 1934. It replaced the Curtiss Condor as America's standard airliner. It had fourteen seats.

A larger version, the Douglas Sleeper Transport, or D.S.T., provided berths for fourteen people, with separate dressing rooms for men and women, each with wash-basins and running water. As a day-plane this was known as the DC-3 and carried twenty-one passengers. Both the DC-2 and DC-3 cruised at 190 mph.

In 1940, 80 per cent. of the airliners on scheduled services in the United States were DC-3s. Known as the Dakota, it was the main Allied short-haul transport aircraft during the war and was used by airlines for many years after 1945.

Douglas DC-4 Skymaster

This was the Allies' main long-haul transport plane during the war. Introduced in 1943, it had a crew of six and carried forty-two passengers. After the war it was operated by many of the world's airlines.

The DC-6 was a stretched and pressurised version of the DC-4.

Douglas DC-6B

A development of the DC-6, it went into service in 1951 and remained in production until 1958. The DC-6B was a very economical aeroplane; it achieved lower costs per seat-mile than any other piston-engined aircraft. It had accommodation for sixty to a hundred passengers.

Fokker F.XVIII

In service by 1932, this three-engined aircraft took fourteen passengers at a speed of 150 mph. It was a fast aircraft for its day and well suited to medium-distance flights, both in Europe and America.

Handley Page 0/400

The first aeroplane to receive a British Certificate of Airworthiness (1 May 1919). The H.P. 0/400 was a civil conversion of a twin-engined heavy bomber. Thirty-four of the forty-three converted were registered in Britain and were all owned by the manufacturers, who had a subsidiary, Handley Page Air Transport Ltd, to operate scheduled services and charters.

The first conversion had no windows, but the later version, the 0/7, had a windowed cabin for fourteen passengers.

Handley Page H.P. 42

An all-metal biplane. A slow (95 mph) aircraft brought into service in 1931 and famous in its time for its high standards of furnishing, quietness and meals. There were two versions, the H.P. 42E or Eastern, for the India and South Africa routes, and the H.P. 42W or Western, for Europe. The passenger cabins were placed fore and aft, with the central section near the engines given over to a baggage hold and to lavatories.

The Eastern model carried twenty-four passengers, the Western thirty-eight.

Junkers G.31

One of the most successful European transport aircraft of the 1920s. A low-wing, three-engined monoplane, it carried a crew of two and sixteen passengers. It was of all-metal construction and had a very good reputation for safety and reliability among the airlines which operated it.

Lockheed Vega

A high-wing, single-engined monoplane of wooden construction, introduced in 1927, which had considerable influence on the subsequent design of aircraft. It did much to prove the value of a stressed-skin structure, by allowing a more slender fuselage and saving weight and material. It cruised with a pilot and six passengers at 100–135 mph.

Lockheed Electra

The Electra, the Douglas DC-1 (of which only one flew) and the Boeing 247 all flew for the first time in 1933–34. 'These three machines, and their immediate progeny, revolutionised the whole sphere of air transport. The dominant features of these first machines were: (a) low-wing, all-metal, monocoque monoplane construction; (b) two powerful, well-cowled and supercharged air-cooled radial engines mounted in the wings, allowing level flight on either engine alone in an emergency; (c) variable-pitch propellers; (d) retractable undercarriage; and (e) wing-flaps, which allowed of increased wing-loading with a low starting speed.'[3] The Electra cruised at 200 mph; it carried ten passengers and a crew of two.

Short S.17 Kent

The Kent was designed for operation on the Mediterranean section of the Britain–India route. The first, *Scipio*, made its maiden flight in 1931. It had four engines and cruised at about 100 mph. In the passenger cabin there was accommodation for sixteen people, in four rows of seats with folding tables. The seats had air cushions, which could be used as life-jackets in an emergency.

Short Empire Flying-Boat

An all-metal, four-engined monoplane, brought into service in 1936, with a range of 800 miles and a cruising speed of 165 mph. It had accommodation for twenty-four passengers and a heavy load of mail and baggage. One of these flying-boats, *Caledonia*, flew the North Atlantic in 1937, without a payload.

Sud-Aviation S.E. 210 Caravelle

One of the most successful and most beautiful of all post-war airliners, the Caravelle went into service in 1959 and was subsequently sold to many of the world's airlines, as a medium-haul aircraft. Accommodation was provided for eighty tourist-class passengers.

Vickers Viscount

The first production model flew in 1952. It had forty-seven seats, five abreast. The Viscount, the first turboprop aeroplane to operate a commercial passenger service, was one of the milestones in civil air transport. It was the first British aircraft to be sold in any quantity in America and went into service with airlines all over the world.

Vickers VC-10

Introduced by BOAC in 1964, to carry 115 passengers in the mixed-class version, 135 in the all-economy class.

The larger Super VC-10, brought into service in 1965, took up to 163 passengers. A very quiet, stable aircraft, and popular with passengers for these reasons.

INDEX

Index